coolcamping

kids

Clover Stroud,

Jonathan Knight, Andrea Oates, Alexandra Tilley Loughrey

with additional contributions by Sophie Dawson and Keith Didcock

The publishers assert their right to use
Cool Camping as a trademark of Punk Publishing Ltd.

Cool Camping: Kids
First edition published in the United Kingdom in 2009 by
Punk Publishing Ltd
3 The Yard
Pegasus Place
London
SE11 5SD

www.punkpublishing.co.uk
www.coolcamping.co.uk

A catalogue record of this book is available from the British Library.

ISBN 978-0-9552036-9-5

10 9 8 7 6 5 4 3 2

Printed in Singapore

introduction

Parents. We know you love holidays. But chances are, since the kids arrived the very concept of holidays has been redefined. Tears, tantrums and tiredness can mean an exhausting experience for everyone, leaving you in need of – well, another holiday.

Luckily, camping and children go together like marshmallows and hot chocolate. The idea of racing around in the outdoors, making dens, making friends, getting muddy and crashing under the stars is, quite frankly, far more agreeable than a week at a hotel or at Aunt Mary's. And as your kids busy themselves with worms and frisbees and fairies, not only does it take the pressure off you, but actually witnessing them have so much fun is one of the great, underrated pleasures of being a parent.

Picking a campsite that will keep you and your children happy, however, is not always as straightforward as it might seem; children rather like adults, bring with them a long list of their own specific demands. It is with this in mind that we have put together this newest addition to the *Cool Camping* series, designed and written specifically for you and the children in your life. We have steered clear of the big corporate sites with chicken-in-a-basket and fruit machines in the clubhouse, wave machines in the swimming pool and karaoke until dawn. Your children would have probably loved that, but we have a hunch that you might not. Instead we have picked a stellar cast of some of the most family-friendly sites on offer in the country, all of which exemplify the certain free-spirited sense of adventure that *Cool Camping* is all about.

All of the sites in this book have been tried and tested by our own children: everyone from newborn babes-in-arms to surly teenagers has given our selection their very own version of a thumbs-up. We think that you and your children, whatever their age, are going to love it, too.

We want you to have the most fun possible with your children, wherever you are camping, so we have given you a thorough section for each site detailing all the practical aspects of your holiday. This includes extensive details about onsite and offsite fun, with listings for local attractions that children are bound to enjoy. And because this is the UK, we've included an 'If it Rains' section, too, so even if it is chucking it down, you should be able to find a nearby castle or two to cavort in until the weather brightens up again.

In the name of serious research, we've tested the best places for local home-made ice cream, the tastiest fish and chips and the most luscious pick-your-own strawberries, to add to the Food & Drink sections. If you are already a fan of the *Cool Camping* books then you'll probably be a pretty independently minded traveller anyway, but because we want you and your family to be safe, we've included a Nanny State Alert section too, briefly outlining any potential hazards you should be aware of.

Part of the pleasure of camping with children is dispensing with the domestic clutter of everyday life. Without sounding too Zen about it, there's a purity to camping that's hard to replicate in 'normal' life, giving you time to completely connect with your children, rather than having to worry about what you are going to put into their packed lunches, whether or not they have learnt for their spelling tests and whether they've got nits or not.

The focus of 'all-in-this-together' fun is food and mealtimes, so we've included a cooking section with some yummy treats you can easily put together on a BBQ or campfire, and which your children will love to help out with, too.

There's also a games section, so you can create your own fun onsite, and we've picked a selection of our favourite festivals that are just as enjoyable for kids as they are for parents. Finally, we've assembled a list of the best residential kids' camps in the country, so even if you're chained to a hot keyboard during the summer, there's no reason why your children shouldn't be having fun around a campfire.

And because we've chosen a wide geographical spread, whichever part of the country you are in, we're pretty sure you'll find something in *Cool Camping: Kids* that you and your children will love.

A few final words to those undecided readers that haven't tried camping before – just give it a go! The worst that could happen is a weekend of wet weather and a wasted few quid. But on the other hand, it might just be your best ever holiday together – and the start of a great, new family adventure…

Happiest Camping!

campsite locator

ABERDEEN

EDINBURGH

GLASGOW

NEWCASTLE   SUNDERLAND

LEEDS   HULL

MANCHESTER

LIVERPOOL

DERBY   NOTTINGHAM

SHREWSBURY   LEICESTER

BARMOUTH

BIRMINGHAM   NORWICH

ABERYSTWYTH

FISHGUARD

HAY-ON-WYE

MILFORD HAVEN

SWANSEA

CARDIFF   BRISTOL

MINEHEAD   LONDON

DOVER

BOURNEMOUTH   BRIGHTON

NEWQUAY

ST IVES

PLYMOUTH   FALMOUTH

9

1　2

3　4

cool camping top 5

Judging for the Top 5 was mostly sensible and well-mannered. Only one judge ended up on the naughty step and lollipops were awarded for good behaviour. Thanks go to Jimmy Joe (aged eight), Dolly (five) and Milini (nine months).

There's magic at Noongallas. It might be its sheltered valley location with the sea in the distance or it could be the gloriously idiosyncratic and relaxed way that the site is run. Maybe you'll find the magic down by the stream, among the ancient beech trees. We're not sure. We just know that there's magic there.

With free camping for musicians and communal campfires, Wowo's free-thinking/wild-camping philosophy has earned them a top spot.

This gorgeous working farm site, nestled in the Dovey Valley, is studded with special spots for kids to play. And the beach is just down the road.

An adventure playground and a rafting pond are just the start of the thrills at Fisherground. When you want some seaside fun, hop on the steam train.

Go 'bush' and camp under a tarp in the middle of an ancient wood. No electricity here, just the sound of twigs snapping as animals scuttle around.

We love the fact that you can pitch your tent at the end of the farm track, with great sea views, but the sugary delights of the seaside town of Cromer are just a short walk away, too.

campsites at a glance

a mum's guide

Kids just love camping. There are few phrases that elicit more delight than 'let's go camping'! 'Want some chocolate?' might come close second!

the best fun

You'd be hard pressed to find a child that doesn't jump at the chance to forgo baths, cook on campfires and spend the night sleeping in a field. Whether you are entertaining your own children, or some you've borrowed for the weekend, camping is the best fun that children and grown-ups can have together. And the great thing is that it doesn't really need that much planning in advance, doesn't have to cost very much and pretty much anyone can do it.

reconnecting with kids

Breaking out of the normal routine of everyday life is also a brilliant way to reconnect with your children. And children really love the fact that, for a few days, you can all kick back and dispense with those phrases that drive us all mad: 'If you don't put your shoes on now we're going to miss the bus/Where's your book bag?/You didn't forget your lunch box again did you?/Is that the time? We're going to be late' that govern most parents' and children's lives. Camping and children are a match made in heaven – just keep a few basic rules in mind and you'll have some very, very happy, fun-sized campers on your hands.

cutting the clutter

We don't want to start *Cool Camping: Kids* with a long list of complicated items for you to rush out and buy. Camping isn't about a retail experience: it's about a real experience. Of course, if you want to go to a camping shop and spend a hefty sum on lots of plasticky nylon bits of camping equipment then go ahead; there's no doubt such retail therapy can be a lot of fun. Just remember that it's not strictly necessary and it's certainly not essential. Camping is all about cutting a lot of clutter out of life. So break free from the screen addiction that dominates our lives, and leave the plastic at home. Of course you can, if you are very well organised, equip each child with a torch, a disposable camera and a backpack full of favourite toys and books, but it might be much more sensible to reckon on the fact that they'll probably lose all those things the moment they get out of the car.

getting your tent legs

A happy camping trip should be framed by the experience of getting out into a beautiful part of the country, perhaps somewhere you've never visited before, throwing up a tent, perhaps borrowed, and then getting down to some serious fun with your kids.

It's as simple as that: home-made fun, like home-made food, is our favourite variety. As well as saving money, cutting back on kit will make your trip a lot less stressful. Squeezing everything you own, plus the kitchen sink, into your car is probably not that much fun for you, or your family. There are a few basic things to bring, or to do, when you are planning a camping trip with children. If you're virgin campers, then it's probably best to borrow kit and head out for a night or two, not too far from home. This way you can work out exactly what you need to take for a longer trip. Don't start your inaugural trip with a 10-hour drive to some far-flung spot, because camping close to home is best until you really get your tent legs: long car trips are tiring, and wherever you live, there are tip-top campsites nearby.

choosing a site

When it comes to choosing a site, remember that pre-warned is pre-armed. Find out what facilities are available beforehand. We all have different tastes, and so do our children, and while some kids will love the lack of boundaries of the more basic sites, others will respond very positively to play facilities and spanking-clean showers being laid on.

Try to arrive at your site in plenty of time before dark, so that your children have time to orientate themselves, explore new surroundings and perhaps even make a new friend or two. Pitching a tent in the dark, while trying to placate hungry children who've spent the day in the car, isn't a particularly good start to your holiday. Arriving just after lunch, perhaps having stopped for a picnic on the way, is ideal; you can then choose a lovely spot, get your camp sorted out and be cheffing up a tasty teatime treat by late afternoon. You might even be able to fit in a trip to the seaside/run through the woods/walk on the moor as well.

safety first

You'll probably find that your children will make friends, fast, with your site neighbours. Free from adult social hang-ups, kids eye each other up and get stuck into a game of football pretty quickly. Make sure you've checked out the site beforehand, so that you are aware of any cliff-top paths or meandering streams, and know exactly how close the site is to the nearest road. We don't go in for huge municipal sites in this book, so if you're staying on a site listed here, we hope that it'll be a small, friendly site with lots of other

things you'll need

■ Tent, sleeping bags, torch, mallet, sharp knife, plates, pillow, towels, fish slice, kettle, pan and a couple of forks are the bare essentials.

■ If you forget something, don't panic. What you can't borrow from other campers, you can improvise. Forgotten your plates? Use a slice of bread instead. Forgotten your pillow? Stuff some clothes into a T-shirt. Forgotten your camping stools? An upturned bucket or an old log works wonders. It's not rocket science, and your kids will love the fun of invention.

■ The only thing you should really worry about forgetting is the tent. And tent pegs. Inventing those might be one challenge too far.

children for yours to play with. Having said that, it's easy to lose sight of a child, fast, between tents. Camping should give your kids a chance to push the boundaries a bit, in a safe environment, but the younger your kids are, the more nerve-wracking this can be. Knowing about potential hazards can help you relax and make you feel less of a headless chicken when you're squawking round the site trying to locate them for tea.

cooking up a storm

Campfire cooking, or on a BBQ, is one of the great delights of camping with kids. If you're lucky enough to find a site where you can have a fire, educate your children to respect the flames. Children and fires are a dangerous combination, but part of the pleasure of camping is that it gives them a chance to learn practical skills that they might be missing in normal life. Lots of us don't have open fires at home, but being able to light and understand a proper fire is a handy life skill. Teach them to cook on that fire, and you might have a budding camp chef on your hands. But whether they are cooking mackerel or toasting marshmallows, teaching them how to respect a fire is a lot more useful than banning them from going anywhere near it. And there are few things more pleasurable in life than sitting round a glowing campfire with your kids, drinking hot chocolate.

getting a lie-in

Don't get your knickers in a twist if your children break their usual curfew. That's half the fun of camping. And take consolation from the fact that if they are knackered in the morning, you might get an extra half hour in your sleeping bag.

wet-weather fun

We know that our great British weather can make or break a camping trip and we really hope that you're camping under glorious sunny skies, but if you aren't, don't despair, as certain strategies can help you cope. A bit of pre-trip research, checking out the forecast and, if it's looking grim, genning up on local museums, castles, activity centres, swimming pools and cinemas, will be time well spent. If you're feeling energetic, brave the rain and relish the fact that you can run around on an empty beach, where you would have been getting wet anyway.

keeping dry

One of the first rules of scouts is that in wet weather you must keep your top half dry and there's no need to worry about your legs. A mac over shorts and wellies is a good combo: long trousers stay wet all day, but skin dries in no time. It's always nice to make your tent cosy, but it's essential when the weather's grim. An extra blanket under sleeping bags will keep kids warmer than one on top, as cold comes up through the ground, and have a no-shoes rule in the tent. The last thing you want is to curl up in a sleeping bag coated with mud. It's also a good rule to keep one set of dry clothes for each child down their sleeping bag. And when packing, you can never take too many socks. But don't let rain spoil your fun; remember that your children probably mind about it a lot less than you do. Most children relish the anarchy of wet weather, and its mud-sliding opportunities.

take a play tent?

Packing a football or rounders bat means you've always got a game handy for your children to occupy themselves with. Board games and cards are useful for wet weather, but fiddly little counters and pieces will quickly get lost. Wink murder (see p55) is probably much simpler, and it doesn't cost a penny. If your sleeping tent isn't capacious, why not take along a little extra tent for playing in, especially if your children are small? It can become a base for games and means that muddy or wet children don't sit on top of their lovely dry, clean bedding. It also gives them a sense of having their own space, and can easily become a Wendy house, space rocket, magic castle or witches' den, depending on what mood your children are in.

Most of all, have fun. Camping is all about spending time together: cooking together, playing together, and at the end of the day, snuggling up together. It's that simple.

Clover

reviewer and camping mum

---

last but not least...

■ It's easy to forget...water container, towels, kettle, pillow, corkscrew.
■ Camping will be easier with...fold-up chairs, wind-up torch, knife, bin bags, chocolate.

noongallas

If you happened to see a real-live hobbit sitting on a grassy knoll at Noongallas, we really wouldn't be at all surprised. This site is full to the brim with fairy glens and mystical glades, where you can make camping magic all of your own.

There's something a little magical about the owner John Line and his campsite, the curiously and wonderfully named Noongallas. JRR Tolkien, famed author of *Lord of the Rings*, would have probably loved it here, and the two of them could have traded their expert knowledge, too.

John can tell you, for example, how many times the fledglings in the dance hall have hatched. He might then show you the best place to pick chanterelle mushrooms (which sell for a small fortune in a fancy deli), and he will help you find the footpath through nearby Trevaylor Woods, where beech trees hang over a bubbling stream.

And the site, sitting on croft land, is pretty special, too, nestled at the edge of a fairly steep site divided into five fields by gorse hedges and waist-high bracken. It's the perfect spot for children to shake off term-time traumas, and the fact that families tend to stay onsite during the day tells you a lot about how convivial and peaceful it is.

Musicians love it here, and you'll often hear a didgeridoo or guitar around the campfire of an evening. Ask John what he likes best about running the site and he'll chuckle and tell you that it's because it makes him feel like he's on holiday all the time. One night here, and you can see why.

noongallas

The Upside With the sea in the distance and fields surrounding you, there's a real sense of space and harmony on the site, assisted by John's very idiosyncratic entertainment.

The Downside The facilities might be a touch too wild for some.

The Facilities Unmarked pitches are scattered across 5 fields. There are flat alcoves and terracing to make pitching easier, as the field is on a slope. There are 2 clean, basic showers and 6 loos in a block (male and female). John provides a washing-up sink that he describes as 'quaint', so don't expect spanking-new facilities, but a mellow, low-impact site. There's a recycling area.

Onsite Fun Gangs of happy children roam the site, and this is a place that families return to again and again. There's a stream running through a mystical glade at the bottom of the field, where children lose track of the day creating camps and making dams. There's a gloriously dilapidated dance hall onsite; you'll find a party in full swing most evenings.

Offsite Fun The best local beach is at Treen. There are another 2 beaches at Long Rock and Marazion, and at the beach at Porthcurno you might even see a dolphin. Penzance is almost at the bottom of the hill. There are fake pirate ships to explore, but don't expect non-stop entertainment here. Trevarno Gardens (01326 574282; www.trevarno.co.uk) are worth a visit. At Gweek there's the National Seal Sanctuary (01326 221361; www.sealsanctuary.co.uk), guaranteed to tug at a few heart strings. Head southwest and you'll find the famous, rather fabulous, Minack Open Air Theatre (01736 810181; www.minack.com).

If it Rains Little ones will enjoy a trip to Dairy Land Farm World near Newquay (01872 510246; www.dairylandfarmworld.com), where there are plenty of amusements. Don't expect sulky teenagers to be impressed. Take them to Future World at Goonhilly (0800 679593; www.goonhilly.bt.com), an interactive exhibition that lets you have a glimpse of life in a hundred years' time.

Food & Drink There's an ice-cream shop on the bridge at Newlyn called Jelberts, and ices there are fantastic. There isn't a decent pub within walking distance, and most campers choose communal campfire cooking, but if you don't mind a drive, the Victoria Inn at Perranuthnoe (01736 710309; www.victoriainn-penzance.co.uk), is very good, if pricey. For reasonable pub grub try the Newlyn Meadery (01736 365375) for chicken and chips and a decent pint. Failing that, buy a bit of haddock at Tesco in Penzance and ask John for his truly delicious chowder recipe.

Nanny State Alert At the bottom of the hill in the trees there's a little stream.

Getting There Follow the A30 from Hayle through Cockwells and Whitecross to Crowlas. At a crossroads after the pub turn right. Follow the road through Ludgvan and bear left after the sign to Vellanoweth. This road runs parallel to the A30 for 2 miles, when you come to Gulval Churchtown. Do not bear left at the church, but pass it on your left. You will soon come to a junction signed to the B3311. Turn left to Penzance, then immediately right, signposted 'Rosemorran and Polkinghorne'. Noongallas is just over a mile up the narrow lane.

Public Transport Train to Penzance, walk 2 miles to the site, or catch the bus (towards New Mill) which stops near the site, or just hop in a taxi.

Open August (licence applied for, for longer).

The Damage £5 per adult a night; £2.50 per kid.

Noongallas, Gulval, Nr Penzance, Cornwall TR20 8YR

| t | 01736 366698 | w | www.noongallas.com | 1 | on the map |

westerley

A faraway field, a fire and a friendly farmer. And that story of the Emperor's new clothes. Everyone came out to see him parading through the town, and they clapped and cheered, even though he had nothing on!

Do you remember that traditional children's story about the Emperor's new clothes? Well, this site, Westerley, is rather like that. We love it even though there's actually nothing there. And that's quite a rare phenomenon in this justifiably popular part of Cornwall – the coast around St Ives is pretty-much heaving with places to pitch your tent. If, that is, you want to stay on a characterless municipal site with tent wall to tent wall, bingo and all-night karaoke. At *Cool Camping*, that's not our idea of fun.

But, in fact, we do like Westerley a lot, because although it's essentially just a field, it's well set back from the road and the beach is just a walk away, so you can leave the masses of Babylon behind. Dare we say this? But the fact that it's so basic actually makes it feel rather exclusive – in a funny sort of way. And there's also the not-inconsiderable fact that the farmer, Mr Stevenson, is a bit of a diamond, who really wants everyone to have a thoroughly good time. He'll deliver logs to your tent if you want to have a little fire and has been spotted helping the uninitiated and newcomers struggling with their guy ropes.

Even the Emperor couldn't complain at that, now, could he?

westerley

The Upside Your kids will be within sight all the time, but there's enough room for ball games and fun. And the beach is only a walk away.

The Downside It might be a little too basic for first-time campers.

The Facilities This site consists of a couple of fields, so you can pitch wherever you want. There are 2 showers and 2 toilets, and some basic washing-up sinks.

Onsite Fun There's nothing onsite for children as such, but there's a lot of space to run around in, and you don't have to worry too much about traffic. There are a few geese to feed, and there are plans to expand to pygmy goats, rabbits and a Shetland pony as well.

Offsite Fun Westerley's surrounded by some lovely parts of Cornwall, including cracking beaches. You can get to Carbis Bay Beach down the lane and along a footpath. Porth Kidney Sands is a fan-shaped beach between Carbis Bay and the Hayle estuary, about 6 miles away. St Ives isn't far, and the beaches there are great, including Porthgwidden, Porthmeor and Clodgy Point. You can hire ponies at Penhalvean riding school, a 10-minute walk from the campsite. Find out about seal rescue at the Seal Sanctuary at Gweek (01326 221361; www.sealsanctuary.co.uk).

If it Rains Paradise Park (01736 751020; www.paradisepark.org.uk) bird sanctuary is open most of the year. There's also a Jungle Barn for indoor play. At Trenhayle Maze (01736 755631; www.maize-maze.com) you can lose yourself, but hopefully not the kids, in Maize Raiders. There's also a maize maze, crazy golf, go-karts, train rides, trampolines, assault course and pedal tractors. If the weather's really dire get underground at Geevor Tin Mine (01736 788662; www.geevor.com) or Poldark Tin Mine (01326 573173; www.poldark-mine.co.uk).

Food & Drink The Countryman, at the end of the lane, does cream teas and is only a 10-minute walk away. Bill and Flo's Farm Shop (01736 798885) in Lelant is good, especially for local cheese and honey. The nearest supermarket is in Carbis Bay. Head to the seafront in St Ives for the best fish and chips. The Sloop Inn (01736 796584; www.sloop-inn.co.uk) on the harbour is nice, and the Cornish Deli (01736 795100) is great for local produce.

Nanny State Alert Watch the main road at the top of the track – cars go pretty fast along it.

Getting There From the A30, take the bypass sign to St Ives when you get to Hayle roundabout. At the next roundabout turn right towards St Ives. Wyevale Garden Centre is on your right. Go to the second mini roundabout past the garden centre and take a sharp left (signposted 'Tyringham Arms, the Countryman and Balnoon Inn'). Follow this road for about 3 miles, until you come to the Balnoon Inn on your right. 45 metres past the inn there is a lane on your right (signposted 'Balnoon'). Go up the lane and the site is 650 metres along on the left-hand side, just past the white bungalow.

Public Transport Head to St Ives on the train and catch the 914 bus towards Threemilestone, hopping off at Balnoon. Then walk to the campsite.

Open August, but application has been made for a licence to extend this.

The Damage £6 per adult and £2 per child aged 3–10 and £4 aged 10–14; dogs go free.

Westerley Campsite, Balnoon, St Ives, Cornwall TR26 3JH

| t 01736 794853 | w www.westerleycampsite.co.uk | on the map |

higher pentreath farm

Beach, beach, beach. It's all about the beach.
And what a very lovely beach it is, too – all big and
golden and sandy – just crying out for an energetic
game of kiss-chase, kick-the-can or frisbee.
And did we mention the beach?

In a county of pretty good beaches, Praa Sands is right up there, waving its blue flag with pride and cleaning its own sands every day with a gentle tide. Its wide, flat reach and safe waters mean it's popular with families; the reliable waves are popular with surfer-dads, while the athletic surfers and bronzed lifeguards are popular with the mums. Yes, it's a popular old place, but there's plenty of room for everybody.

From its bird's-eye vantage point above all this hubbub, Higher Pentreath Farm surveys the day. It watches the crack-of-dawn surfers, the pre-breakfast dog-walkers and the café coffee-sippers. It watches the day-trippers come and go and the evening joggers to and fro. And as the setting sun lights the bay with the golden tones of summer evenings, those lucky campers at Higher Pentreath Farm need only to step outside their tents to appreciate this special cove.

The three fields that form the site offer increasingly better views the higher up you go; but the payback of this hillside location is the sloping ground, so be prepared. It's also worth noting that the slope to the beach makes it quick and easy to get to, but exponentially harder to get back from. Better just to sit and watch it all from your camping chair. Another beer anyone?

higher pentreath farm

The Upside The view, the beach, the excuse that it's just too difficult to get back up that hill.

The Downside It can get pretty crowded in summer, and the facilities aren't the greatest.

The Facilities The main block has 12 toilets and 4 showers for ladies and just 1 shower, 3 toilets plus some urinals for the gents. But don't feel like you're the victims of sexism here, guys, as there's a smaller block behind the farmhouse with 3 toilets and another shower. They can get a bit mucky during busy times, so have your flip-flops to hand and spare loo roll, though rumour has it this situation is improving. There's also a washing machine and ironing board available in the laundry room, 3 large sinks for dishwashing, electrical hook-ups and waste-disposal facilities.

Onsite Fun Loads of lovely space in the main field to run around and around and around in – till everyone's really dizzy.

Offsite Fun The beach. Surfboards are available to hire and there are rock pools at either end of the mile-long beach. A pub, café and beach shop are all within easy reach.

If it Rains Flambards (01326 573404; www.flambards.co.uk) in nearby Helston is a vast adventure ride, activities and exhibitions attraction. The rides are outdoors, but the popular Victorian Village experience is inside, along with play areas and a hands-on science experience. A family-of-4 saver ticket costs £42.40. A more cultured alternative would be the Tate – plus the cafés, restaurants and shops – at St Ives (01736 796226; www.tate.org.uk/stives), about 20 minutes' drive from here.

Food & Drink The Sandbar Pub and Restaurant (01736 763516; www.sandbarpraasands.co.uk) is just off the beach and has incredible views. Relax with a beer or healthy smoothie while the kids play pool or air hockey; then tuck into an organic wrap, baguette or fresh beach bite. Further afield, the Bay Restaurant, Café and Gallery (01736 366890; www.bay-penzance.co.uk) in Penzance has a constantly changing menu featuring freshly caught fish and crabs from the local market, and it also boasts its own gallery and great balcony views.

Nanny State Alert Make sure the bicycle brakes work before spinning off down the hill to the beach.

Getting There From the A30, take the turning for the A394. After approximately 5 miles, turn right onto Pentreath Lane and follow the road for almost half a mile. Look out for the sign for 'Higher Pentreath' by the second track on the right. Reception is just down the track on the right.

Public Transport Take a train to Penzance then hop onto a First Western National bus 2, 2A or 2B to Praa Sands. If the bus driver's a good 'un you may be lucky enough to get dropped off at the campsite.

Open Easter/1st April (whichever comes first) until the end of October.

The Damage Family of 4 with car and large tent costs £11.50 a night. Dogs are welcome at no extra charge, if kept on leads. Electric hook-ups available for £3 a night.

Higher Pentreath Farm, Praa Sands, Penzance, Cornwall TR20 9TL

t   01736 763222

3 on the map

arthur's field

With three little beaches and a heritage farm outside
your tent, it's not hard to see why kids adore
Arthur's Field. Just be ready for hissy fits at going-home
time. Well, you can always come back next year.

You could call site-owners Debbie and Richard Walker's relationship with Arthur's Field something of a love affair. And a pretty passionate one at that. When they first visited the site with their two young sons, to surf and explore the south coast at the point where Cornwall dips her heel into the dazzling waters of Falmouth Bay, the field was run by Victor Barry. He's an inspirational local legend who harvested his crops using shire horses pulling vintage machinery.

The site is low-impact; hardly surprising since Victor was pushing organic farming decades before Jamie Oliver was even a twinkle in his mum's eye. One visit, and the Walkers were in love and moved in. Sitting on the cliff-top just above Treloan Cove, and within strolling distance of postcard-pretty Portscatho, Arthur's Field is a site that stressed-out urbanite campers can only dream about.

Victor can boast of producing a loaf from his own crops with absolutely no carbon footprint, so it seems only right that once you have pitched your tent, there's really no need to get into your car again until going-home time comes around. Problem is, you'll probably never want to go home at all. Just like Debbie and Richard, you'll end up wanting to live the dream.

arthur's field

The Upside A hop and a skip across a field and you can jump straight into the sea, with fantastic walks along the South West Coastal Path.

The Downside The site isn't huge and can get cramped peak season.

The Facilities 57 pitches, all with hook-ups, are spread over 1 field. There are 11 showers, including 3 family, and 6 sinks, including 1 at kid-height, so Junior has no excuse for not washing up his hot-chocolate mug. BBQs permitted in trays.

Onsite Fun Every morning Debbie rings a bell, Pied Piper-like, and children come running to help her collect eggs and feed the rabbits. In summer the cow's field is mowed to create a football pitch, and there are cricket stumps, too. Unsurprisingly, children are devoted to Arthur's Field and tantrums at going home time are not uncommon.

Offsite Fun There's private access to 3 secluded beaches, all great for swimming, fishing and diving, especially Treloan Cove and Peter's Splosh. Slightly further are Carne and Towan beaches, but worth it for the sand. Porthcurnick beach is walkable from the other side of Portscatho, and seals are regular visitors – both beaches often seem empty after the heaving crowds of Polzeath and Padstow. Portscatho (01872 580989; www.portscathoholidays.co.uk) is a lovely place to spend the afternoon fishing or rock-pooling; if you're lucky you might spot the distant flipping tails of dolphins. Wander along the coastal path from the site and you may see buzzards, badgers and foxes.

If it Rains Don waterproofs and take a ferry from Portscatho to St Mawes. Catch another to Falmouth. The National Maritime Musem (01326 313388; www.nmmc.co.uk) will keep kids amused for hours. The city's not bad for quirky shopping,

especially in charity shops, if you or your teenagers are in urgent need of retail therapy. Local castles include Caerhays Castle (01872 501310; www.caerhays.co.uk), Pendennis Castle (01326 316594; www.english-heritage.org.uk) and St Mawes Castle (01326 270526; www.stmawes.info).

Food & Drink The Walkers organise a family evening twice a week. An Italian lady cooks, or the Walkers knock up old favourites like jacket potatoes and chilli. Tesco will deliver and the Plume of Feathers and the Royal Standard are within walking distance. Locally caught fish lifts their menus above standard pub grub. The Boathouse (01872 580326; www.theboathouse.co.uk), in the village, is nice for cream teas, and you can buy fantastic seafood from Ralph's Shop. Down the road is the Blue Carrot (01872 580942; www.thebluecarrot.co.uk), where you can buy just-picked goodies.

Nanny State Alert The site is within walking distance of the cliffs, so little ones should be accompanied.

Getting There Follow the A3078 until you reach Trewithian. Turn left at 'Treloan Coastal Farm' towards Gerrans and Portscatho. Stay on this road until you reach Gerrans Church square and stop beside the church, opposite the Royal Standard inn. Treloan Lane is marked on the wall and runs directly to Arthur's Field, 300 yards down this lane on the left-hand side.

Public Transport Catch a train or coach to Truro (about 19 miles from the campsite) then take a bus (50/51) towards St Mawes. Hop off at Portscatho and walk from there.

Open All year.

The Damage From £13 (Oct–March, excluding Christmas week), up to £20.50 (late July–3 Sept).

Arthur's Field, Treloan Lane, Gerrans, Nr Portscatho, Roseland Peninsula, Truro, Cornwall TR2 5EF

t 01872 580989   w www.coastalfarmholidays.co.uk   on the map

ruthern valley

Cornwall isn't all about sun, sand and surfing. What about rabbits, woodpeckers, squirrels and trees? Woody, green Ruthern feels a million miles from the bustling Cornish coast, but it's actually only a short drive.

After a nice day on the beach at Polzeath or Rock, surrounded by surfers and Sloanes, Ruthern Valley is somewhere you can escape to, hidden among the green canopy of Cornwall's countryside interior.

Close to Bodmin Moor, this secluded, beguiling little site is humming with wildlife, so children can have plenty of fun spotting rabbits and squirrels, and budding ornithologists can look out for woodpeckers a-pecking and hear owls a-hooting. Having said that, they'll probably enjoy feeding the chickens just as much, too. It's a top location, with the wild delights of Land's End an hour or so away, and Bodmin Moor, the perfect place for stomping around with children, as you regale them with heady stories about smugglers and highwaymen, isn't far. Or you could cycle to Padstow for a crabbing session on the quay and perhaps a slap-up portion of Mr Stein's famous fish and chips, which is a pretty-much perfect way to while away an afternoon.

Grogley Woods are close to the site and lovely for shady walks. So, at the end of a busy day, when you've had your fill, and more, of sun, sea and sand, what could be better than the peaceful, leafy shade of Ruthern Valley?

ruthern valley

The Upside In the middle of Cornwall, this is a magic place to escape the beach crowds.

The Downside The statics are ugly and if you hit a wet week, overhanging trees make the whole experience quite a damp one.

The Facilities 29 beautifully flat pitches, 6 with hook-ups, spread over 4 camping areas. The 5 most secluded pitches are in the wood. There are 3 solar-powered showers and 2 washing-up sinks. Laundry facilities include 2 washers, 2 dryers and an ironing board, so no excuse for campers looking crumpled. There are also 'camping pods'; timber-built insulated huts for 2 adults and 2 kids; great if the weather gets dodgy and you feel like a little TLC. Lambs'-wool insulation makes autumn camping positively cosy.

Onsite Fun Fun is of the tent-made variety, but there's a small play area and a football space. In the woods there are lots of places for making dens. The family keeps pigs and chickens, which children can help to feed.

Offsite Fun Part of the appeal of Ruthern Valley is its proximity to the Camel Trail (01872 327310; www.cornishlight.co.uk), a disused railway track running 16 miles from Wadebridge to Padstow. It's a great route for walking or cycling. Hire bikes at Bodmin Bikes (01208 731192; www.bodminbikes.co.uk) or Bridge Bike Hire, Wadebridge (01208 813050; www.bridgebikehire.co.uk); both have children's bikes, bike seats and trailer bikes. There's a riding stable at St Breward (01208 851500).

If it Rains Pencarrow House (01298 841369; www.pencarrow.co.uk) is fun for a day out, and the Peacock Café does decent home-cooked food and also has a playpit, rabbits, guinea pigs and peacocks. Newquay Zoo (01637 873342; www.newquayzoo.org.uk) is bearable and the Blue Reef Aquarium (01637 878134; www.bluereefaquarium.co.uk) is good, as well as doing great-value kids' packed lunches in the café. Tintagel Castle (01840 770663; www.tintagelweb.co.uk) is an interesting place to go and find out about King Arthur. The Bodmin and Wenford Railway (08451 259678; www.bodminandwenfordrailway.co.uk) is excellent if you fancy a nostalgic day out.

Food & Drink There's a small shop onsite for basic groceries and local produce. They sell award-winning curries from the Little Cornish Curry Company, Roskilly's ice cream, fresh baguettes and local Rattler cider. Cycle 3 miles along the Camel Trail to the Borough Arms (01208 731118; www.theborougharms.com), which is a child-friendly pub.

Nanny State Alert There's a stream by the site.

Getting There Come down the A30 past Bodmin to Innis Downs to the roundabout for St Austell. Take the slip road off the A30 and turn right at the first roundabout, taking you back over the A30 to the next roundabout. Take the second exit off the roundabout signed for Lanivet (A389). Keep going through Lanivet until you see Presingoll Pottery on the left. Immediately before the pottery turn left, signed for Nanstallon. Turn left again, signed for Ruthern Bridge (chalets), and continue for approximately 2 miles, turning left immediately before the small bridge.

Public Transport Bus sightings are rarer than those of the Beast of Bodmin Moor, so catch a train to Bodmin Parkway and taxi from there.

Open April–Oct.

The Damage From £11.50 per tent for 2 adults plus £2.75 for children. Camping pod: £30–35 per night (2 people). No dogs during July or August.

Ruthern Valley Holidays, Ruthern Bridge, Bodmin, Cornwall PL30 5LU

| t 01208 831395 | w www.ruthernvalley.com | 5 on the map |

cornish tipi

Imagine the atmospheric smell of woodsmoke,
the mouth-watering sizzle of a trout caught fresh from a
glittering aquamarine lake and the sound of your children's
laughter as they play happily outside your tipi. You could almost
be in a *Vogue* fashion shoot.

Camping used to be all about nasty nylon sleeping bags and unpleasantly soggy tents. Then along came the concept of glamorous camping (or, rather, 'glamping'), and suddenly you couldn't move for fashionistas throwing up Alice Temperley-style tipis in the remoter parts of the great British countryside. But what makes Cornish Tipi Holidays a bit different, and, we like to think, a bit special, is that it's the real thing and there isn't a bottle of Coke in sight. Authenticity and longevity are the key words.

Set up in 1997 by Elizabeth Tom and Alan Berry, it was the first commercial tipi campsite in England and over a decade down the line it's still going strong. The site's arranged around the stunning spring-fed lake in the old Tregildrans quarry, and it forms a natural eco-system. Breeding hawks soar through the sky and the tangled edges of the stony paths are a natural haven for moths, butterflies and even perhaps the odd dormouse.

In this wilder-than-wild environment, children can't fail to flourish. No surprise, then, to hear that Alice Temperley herself spent her honeymoon here. Now what on earth would Hiawatha have thought about that?

cornish tipi

The Upside Beautiful tipis, masses of space, a fishing and swimming lake; all within striking distance of some of the north Cornish coast's best beaches.

The Downside Limber up – you're going to have to carry all your own water to your tipi.

The Facilities 40 tipis are scattered around the 16-acre site, with 2 large 'village fields' of 6 and 11 large tipis, interspersed with smaller sites. There are loos and hot showers at either end of the site and a larger shower block, too. Every tipi has a lantern, box of utensils and logs. There are standpipes and water-containers throughout the site. The site's proud to be off the National Grid, so you can really get back to nature here.

Onsite Fun It's easy to spend the day by the lake, messing about in a boat or fishing for trout, but bring your own rods and licence (or buy equipment at Trelawney Garage). Borrow life-jackets from the warden. Fishing is popular, as is cooking the catch on a campfire. As well as the winding paths edged by tumbling blackberries or bright-yellow gorse, and sparkling streams and shady woodland to explore, there are also the larger 'village fields' for children to charge about in, and the 'top village field' has a spectacular totem pole.

Offsite Fun Head to Port Isaac (01208 880200; www.portisaac-online.co.uk), a great place for sea-kayaking, and buying scallops or crabs. Pick up the Camel Trail near Wadebridge (01460 221162; www.cornishlight.co.uk) and explore the 16 miles John Betjeman described as 'the best journey in England'. Lanhydrock House (01208 265950; www.cornwall-calling.co.uk) is a Victorian mansion near Bodmin, with over 50 rooms to explore. On the south coast stop at Charlestown Shipwreck Centre (01726 69897; www.shipwreckcharlestown.com) in the historic china-clay building. You can walk through underground tunnels and there's an exciting collection of dive treasures.

If it Rains Crealy Great Adventure (01841 540276; www.crealy.co.uk) is good for an all-weather family day out. There's also Holywell Bay Fun Park (01637 830095; www.holywellbay.co.uk). North Cornwall Arts (01840 214220; www.art-cornwall.co.uk) runs plenty of children's workshops.

Food & Drink For groceries use the Spar in Delabole (01840 213897). It does fresh pizza most Friday and Saturday nights. You can buy excellent pasties from either Auntie Avice (great egg-and-bacon pie) at St Kew or Cornish Maids in Camelford (01840 212749). The Other Place in Fowey (01726 833636; www.theotherplacefowey.com) does creative fish and chips, including scallops or calamari. For excellent Sunday lunch and good mid-week sandwiches try the Globe Hotel at Lostwithiel (01208 872501).

Nanny State Alert The catch on the gate by the quarry lake is not completely childproof.

Getting There Take the M5 to Exeter then the A30 to Okehampton and Launceston. Turn right onto the A395 to Camelford. Just before Camelford turn right at Collan's Cross onto the B3314 to Delabole. Follow the road out of Delabole for a couple of miles, then turn left for St Teath at the Port Gaverne crossroads. Stay on the road curving around to the right, over an old railway bridge, then take first right before Normansland Cottage, and go down the track.

Public Transport The nearest station is Bodmin Parkway, or fly to Newquay then take a taxi.

Open Mid-March–early Nov.

The Damage A family of 4 or 5 in a large tipi in peak season costs from £555 per week, and from £435 in the off-season. Minimum stay 2 nights.

Cornish Tipi Holidays, Tregeare, Pendoggett, St Kew, Cornwall PL30 3LW

| t | 01208 880781 | w | www.cornishtipiholidays.co.uk | 6 | on the map |

belle tents

Who says that camping has to be about serried ranks of boring beige tents? These stripy beauties look like delicious strawberry Cornettos and make camping here a complete doddle – everything you can think of is already provided. Utter camping bliss!

Poet John Betjeman, synonymous with all things truly 'English' earmarked Cornwall as his favourite place in the entire country and he wrote about it a great deal. He's buried at the church at St Enodoc – for all those campers who wish to pay him homage. So because Cornwall is truly Betjeman-country, it's completely appropriate that you can camp in a bell tent, reading to your children from *A Ring of Bells* (for younger readers), to the distant sound of the bells of St Endellion church. It really is a beautifully beguiling thought.

Belle Tents is a great place for wildlife-spotting, so the budding naturalists in the family can have a field day, particularly in the evenings, when butterflies and moths flit around the wild garden. But however you choose to fill your time during your stay, there's something theatrical about being here. The tents are set up like a medieval encampment, reminding all of times gone by.

Hippies at heart, site owners Laura and Dave make these wonderful tents themselves. Their studio is just beside this sunny, south-westerly-facing site, which is also home to rare-breed cattle and ponies grazing in the fields alongside. A stunning setting that might just inspire you to write some poetry of your own.

belle tents

The Upside The site's large enough for everyone to have their own space, but small enough never to worry about the kids: they're almost certainly making friends in the next-door camp.

The Downside During high season and summer, bookings run for a whole week, and you pay a £10 charge per head per week on top of the tent fees. No pets allowed.

The Facilities The camping field is divided into 3 camps, each containing 2 tents, one with a double and 1 with twin beds, accommodating 4–6 people. Camping is a doddle, as each tent's kitted out with cutlery, firewood, a BBQ and a cooker, with a few essentials such as tea. Campers are asked to bring their own linen, and each camp has a separate high-pressure shower and toilet. There's one large communal fire. At night the site's lit by solar markers, which campers can use as nightlights.

Onsite Fun There's a gorgeous children's tent with formica-topped tables and jam jars stuffed with wild flowers, where children congregate to play, with a wood-burner for chilly evenings. There are games like dominoes and cards, as well as plenty of paper and crayons, a few paperbacks and table football.

Offsite Fun The sandy delights of the north coast are 5 miles away; Tintagel Castle (01840 770328; www.tintagelcastle.co.uk) and beach is great for a day out. Polzeath beach (01208 862003; www.polzeathincornwall.co.uk) is particularly good for surfing, with several different surf schools jostling for space beside ice-cream shops. You can go seal-watching at the Rumps, and dolphins are sometimes seen off New Polzeath. Hire a boat at Bude and row up the canal, which will seem wonderfully quiet after the hoards on the coast. Walk along the river for a picnic, starting in the middle of Camelford, where there's a park with swings.

If it Rains At the Lost Valley (01726 845100) there's a maze, treasure hunt and little train. Carnglaze Caverns (01579 320251; www.carnglaze.com) are worth a visit, with an enchanted dell dotted with bronze fairies and mushrooms. Camelford has several museums, including a Museum of Cycling (01840 212811; www.chycor.co.uk) at the old station at Slaughterbridge.

Food & Drink Each camp has its own garden with edible plants and herbs, and the communal fire often means campers cook together. There's a Co-op, fish-and-chip shop and Chinese take-away in Camelford, and the Masons Arms (01840 213309) does great food, especially local sea bass and mussels. There's also a first-rate fruit-and-veg shop called A1 Fruiterers. The Rising Sun (01566 86636), near Altarnun, has excellent food. There's a good fish shop at Widemouth for mackerel for the barbie.

Nanny State Alert There are horses in the field beside the site.

Getting There From the M5 at Exeter, take the A30 towards Bodmin. Three miles past Launceston take the second exit for the A395 towards North Cornwall and Wadebridge. After 8 miles enter Hallworthy. Carry on towards Camelford for another mile. On the brow of the hill turn left, then go down the hill to a T-junction. Turn left then right up a track (you should see the Belle Tents sign). Continue towards the house with the red-tiled roof.

Public Transport You really do need a car, but those brave enough to try it without need to take a train/coach to Exeter St Davids, then a Greyhound coach to Davidstow Church. Walk from there.

Open End May–3rd week in Sept.

The Damage £45–55 for a tent per night (2–3 people); £85–95 per night (4–6 people).

Belle Tents, Owl's Gate, Davidstow, Camelford, Cornwall PL32 9XY

t 01840 261556   w www.belletentscamping.co.uk   on the map

camping games

Part of the reason why kids love to go camping so much is because it feels like one long party.

Away from all the techno intrusions into almost all areas of our lives, camping encourages a high degree of parent–child interaction. Put bluntly, you can't really escape to the living room to read the Sunday papers, or your office to check your emails and update your Facebook profile.

Chances are that you'll find yourself playing the sort of ridiculous, hilarious and sometimes occasionally humiliating games that you were always desperate for your parents to play with you when you were a child.

There's always plenty of room in every camping trip for the usual ball games like rounders or French cricket, so don't forget to fling bats, balls and rackets – and anything else that you think might be useful – into the boot of your car when you are packing. However, for wet weather (which is bound to happen), when you are confined under canvas, board games and playing cards are worth their weight in gold. But there's also something delightful about home-made games that are just plucked out of the ether.

What follows here is a selection of some of our favourite games. They don't involve a single piece of kit, but they do involve a lot of fun.

letter chaos

Choose a single category, such as animals, girls' names, sweets or food. The first player calls out a single item from that category, and the next player has to use the last letter of that word to make the first letter of the next word. For example, if you choose animals, a round might go like this: horse, elephant, tiger, rhinoceros. You can make the game more complicated for older children, if you like, using more challenging categories, such as rivers or foreign cities. You might even find that you can trick a teenager into doing some geography revision, without him or her even realising it! This is also a good game to play on long car journeys, particularly when you are driving to a far-flung campsite.

scavenger hunt

This is a brilliant game to while away an afternoon on the beach. Devise a list of possible treasures that each child has to go and hunt for. First, agree on a search area around your site, tent or beach-base. For example, the list could include a bottle top, a feather, a piece of sea-smoothed glass, a completely round stone, and so on. Provide each child with a bucket (or an old yogurt pot or similar container) to carry their treasures in, and send them off to hunt for them, while you stretch out with a good book. For the game to last longer, make the items a bit harder to find, like a stone with a hole in it, a starfish or a crab's claw. The winner is the one who has collected the most treasures after an agreed period of time.

kick-the-can

Choose an open space, but ideally with some natural hiding places. The best place is in a wood, or on sand dunes. One person is made 'king'/'queen', and must stand in the middle of the space beside the 'can'. This could be an old bucket or a stump of wood. The king/queen covers their face, counts to 25 and all the players must then hide. The aim is for the players to get close enough to the can to kick it. The king/queen must defend the can (now with eyes uncovered) and try to get a player out by tagging him. Once players are out they wait by the can in 'prison'. The other players then try to free the prisoners by kicking the can without being tagged. The game usually involves some high-speed chases to the can, and a lot of cheering.

wink murder

A good game for a wet afternoon, when you've visited every local castle there is and all anyone wants to do is sit in the tent. Rip up a sheet of paper into as many pieces as there are players. On one piece write the word 'murderer'. Fold the pieces and put them into a hat. Each person (sitting in a circle) takes a piece and checks whether they are the murderer, without letting anyone else see. The murderer then winks surreptitiously at each player, who will then 'die'. The murdered one counts to 10 before dying so that others can't guess who the murderer is. High drama and histrionics are fully permitted from the dying player at this point. The aim of the game is for the murderer to wink each player out without anyone guessing who the murderer is.

sports day

This works best with a large group of people, but even if you are in a small group it's still a lot of fun. If you want you can mark out a start and finish line with a biodegradable line of flour, but you could just do it with things you have lying around onsite, like a skipping rope, a spare guy rope or an anorak. Use your imagination when choosing the sort of heats that you want to have: fiercely competitive running races are a good place to start, but you could quickly graduate to the three-legged race, hopping race, running-backwards race, egg-and-spoon race and the favourite wheelbarrow race. You could race as teams, or individually. Close your sports day with a grand presentation of prizes, maybe in the form of chocolates and sweets.

witch's ring

Mark out a small circle on the ground using flour or a rope (or mark the sand with a stick). Choose one player to be the 'witch'. She (or he) crouchs in the circle while the other players walk around it. The witch then slowly rises and, on reaching full height, shouts 'Here I come!'. She then dashes out and tries to catch another player. Anyone she catches is turned into something of her choice, for example, a dog or a toad and the player has to freeze in that pose. The whole thing is then repeated until all the players have been caught by the witch and she is surrounded by a field full of strange-looking people contorted into silly shapes. Great fun and loads of hilarity!

runnage farm

Recharge your fading batteries by plugging into some serious countryside relaxation. You'll find a sprinkling of campfire magic plus a hearty dose of camping by the river in the very heart of wildest Dartmoor.

Heading into Dartmoor feels a bit like travelling through time and tales, perhaps ending up somewhere between the pages of *The Hound of the Baskervilles*. Much of the land here has successfully spurned modernity's advances, and its middle-of-nowhereness and descending mists give it an air of mystery and adventure; it's bound to stir up even the most sluggish of imaginations.

Runnage Farm is right in the midst of this rolling moorland. Extending over 220 acres, it has been worked by the Coakers since 1843, long before Baker Street's finest sleuth arrived to solve his famous case.

The Coakers are keen to emphasise that running the farm is their priority, but they are happy to offer a small, wild campsite along with a few mod cons. There are no pitches or hook-ups, just two fields next to the river, where campers are free to do as they please. Kids can run around in this magical wilderness, playing Pooh Sticks in the river, looking at the horses and splashing about in the stream.

Any grown-ups who are by now feeling slightly frazzled can unwind to the tranquil sounds of rural peace and calming, flowing water. As a certain pipe-smoking detective would say: 'It's elementary, my dear camper.'

runnage farm

The Upside The excitement of wild-style camping near water, making campfires and barbecuing some of the farm's meaty treats.

The Downside Without a car it's difficult to reach, and Dartmoor weather can be a tad unpredictable.

The Facilities If you don't fancy outdoor camping, there are 3 converted barns. Two are heated and have a cooker, microwave, toaster, kettle, hot water and seating areas. A third is grander, with its own kitchen, large seating area, and separate shower/ toilet cubicles (one ladies', one gents'), there's also heating in winter. The shower block next to the Old Stable (shared with those staying in the converted barns) is equipped with 4 clean toilets and 2 showers. No washing machines or dryers, but you're welcome to use the drying room.

Onsite Fun Splashing along the Walla Brook stream that splits the camping fields, playing hide-and-seek in the forest and toasting marshmallows on a roaring campfire. There's also an orienteering course (depending on time of year and numbers).

Offsite Fun Choose from pony-trekking, canoeing, rock-climbing or hiring bikes from the nearby B&B (£15 per day, £4 an hour; 01822 880332). For littler kids and the young at heart, the Miniature Pony Centre (01647 432400; www.miniatureponycentre.com), between Moretonhampstead and Postbridge, has over 150 animals for kids to meet, as well as offering activities such as egg-collecting and pony-grooming.

If it Rains Enjoy a hearty Devon cream tea in Postbridge or Widecombe, or indulge in a shopping trip to Trago Mills (01626 821111) near Newton Abbot, where they have shops galore as well as heaps of stuff like 'all-weather' skating.

Food & Drink Treat yourselves to Runnage Farm's beefburgers, lamb chops, marinated lamb steaks and scrummy lamb-and-rosemary burgers to whack on the BBQ (let them know what you need in advance). You can also buy freezer-ready packs of meat for a taste of the moors when you get home. The Old Inn at Widecombe (01364 621207) provides a choice-full menu and offers a special children's menu plus half-portions from the adults' menu for the kids.

Nanny State Alert As Runnage is a working farm, parents are encouraged to accompany children (especially younger ones) at all times. Tractors and vehicles constantly trundle along the drive, and some fields are marked 'keep out'. Farm dogs are friendly, but campers are asked not to make a fuss of them, as they need to keep focused on their work.

Getting There Head south along the A38, taking the Newton Abbot exit and follow the A382 all the way to Moretonhampstead, where you can get on the B3212 to Postbridge. Just as you pass the sign welcoming you to Postbridge there's a sharp left signposted to Widecombe. Runnage Farm is about a mile down that road on the left.

Public Transport Catch a train to Exeter, Ashburton or Plymouth and hop on the X38 trans-moor bus service to Postbridge. It's a mile-and-a-bit walk from there.

Open All year, but call to double-check in winter.

The Damage £16 per night for 2 adults with 2 kids aged 3–12. Kids under 3 are free. Dogs cost £2.50 per night and must be on leads. Use of the camping barns is £7.50 per person, per night, or £90/£85 sole use. The Bunkhouse costs £70 per night for either of the 6-bed rooms or £130 for sole use.

Runnage Farm, Postbridge, Yelverton, Devon PL20 6TN

t 01822 880222 　　　w www.runnagecampingbarns.co.uk 　　 on the map

coombe view farm

Branscombe would make the perfect setting for a Famous Five story. A picturesque, uppy-downy village perched on the Jurassic Coast of East Devon, it feels more rural than seaside – a truly unspoiled corner.

With walks aplenty, overlooking a pebbled shore, this is the kind of place where Julian, Anne, Dick, George and Timmy could get seriously stuck into some mischievous adventures.

Shaped like an upright horseshoe, with the beach at the very bottom, Branscombe village has two ends and at one of them you'll find Coombe View Farm Caravan and Camping Site.

This relaxed site has lovely views over the fields – to your left you can see the sea. The main field is a sloped green expanse, with a few static and touring caravans around the edges and a couple of picnic tables dotted about. It's an understated, quiet place that emanates a rural vibe, with inquisitive ponies stretching long necks over the fence to have a nose at their neighbours.

Campers are more than welcome to explore the surrounding land when they are not on the beach. Kids can play games, create Enid Blyton-style escapades and collect wood for campfires in the fields that aren't occupied by animals. And when the sun goes down, the village's Mason's Arms pub is just the spot for a fizzy ginger beer beside the roaring log fire.

coombe view farm

The Upside Stunning rural, campfire-permitting location, with a beach within easy reach.

The Downside The roads leading to the beach aren't exactly pedestrian-friendly and the village may be a bit too low-key for older kids. There are quite strict guidelines on, for example, excessive cycling speeds and hanging out your washing.

The Facilities The site has 4 toilets and just 2 showers – all very basic, but with a good supply of hot water to wash away salty waves and ice-creamy fingers. There's also an outside tap and chemical toilet disposal unit. Please ask the owners if you'd like to have a campfire, so they can let you know the safer places to set them up.

Onsite Fun There's plenty of room for kids to run about and play, and the centre of the main field is the perfect size for a makeshift cricket pitch to keep budding Kevin Pietersens happy.

Offsite Fun Beach time! Long, pebbly and part of the acclaimed Jurassic Coast, Branscombe beach is perfect for stone-skimming, splashing around and swimming in its clean waters. The Sea Shanty Shop and Restaurant (01297 680577; www.theseashanty. co.uk) backs onto the beach, providing tasty snacks, ice creams and beachy paraphernalia. The Donkey Sanctuary (Slade House Farm, Sidmouth; 01395 578222; www.drupal.thedonkeysanctuary.co.uk) is only a couple of miles away, where visitors are encouraged to wander around the fields making a fuss of the donkeys and enjoying the picturesque countryside around the centre.

If it Rains Step 300 years back in time to Branscombe's National-Trust-restored old Forge, Manor Mill and Old Bakery (01392 881691). Watch the traditional handcrafting of ironwork in the only working thatched forge left in the country, then enjoy a cream tea in the Old Bakery, with its old-fashioned baking equipment and open fires (admission £2.60 per adult and £1.30 per child).

Food & Drink If you're still hungry after the cream tea head for the Mason's Arms (01297 680300; www.masonsarms.co.uk) in the village. It has a cosy, log-fire atmosphere, with elderly locals playing dominoes, dogs stretching out under tables and a good selection of tasty pub grub to choose from.

Nanny State Alert Horses in the neigh-bouring fields tend to bite (there are warning signs on the fences) so best keep young hands away. Fields below the campsite are steep. The lanes leading to the beach are pretty narrow, with lots of bends, so take extra care when heading along them on foot.

Getting There Head south down the M5, exit at junction 30 and follow signs for the A3052 towards Sidmouth. Keep going along the A3052 past Sidmouth towards Seaton. There are 3 signed right turn-offs to Branscombe, take the third (the one after Branscombe Cross), and Coombe View Farm is about half a mile down the track on the right.

Public Transport Take the train to Honiton or Exeter, then the 52B stagecoach bus to the Post Office or Triangle in Sidmouth, where you can hop onto the mini 899 bus to Branscombe village hall, then it's uphill from there on in!

Open Mid-March–mid-Oct.

The Damage Family of 4 (kids aged 5–14) and car costs £16–18 per night, depending on season. There's a £6 charge for tents over 150 x 320cm. Dogs £2 per night in high season.

Coombe View Farm, Branscombe, Seaton, Devon EX12 3BT

| t | 01297 680218 | w | www.coombeview.fsnet.co.uk | 9 | on the map |

cloud farm

A truly irresistible spot for kids who are already
hooked on riding and for those who want to give
it a go. There are native Exmoor ponies all around the
farm and you can go riding right from the site's
very own stables.

Devon is a county that is heaving
with campsites, no doubt because
it has one of the most spectacular
bits of coastline in the country.
You'll find that the road out of
Ilfracombe is practically a sea
of tents, all busily jostling for space
beside statics and chicken-and-
chip clubhouses, which bring to
mind a not-so-Happy Valley.

Not surprisingly, we don't really
want to pitch our tent there. So
Cloud Farm comes as a breath of
fresh air. It's in a pretty, self-
contained hamlet surrounded by
the purple haze of the Doone
Valley, with the Badgworthy
Water river on one side.

On the site you will find that there
are two possible areas you can
choose to camp in. You can pitch
either on a strip beside the river or
in the larger field on the hill. The
latter spot is perfect if you feel
the need for a little more space,
peace and quiet.

Because this site is mercifully
free from too many rules and
regulations, it goes without saying,
doesn't it, that Cloud Farm's the
sort of place where you can have
your own campfire – so this is the
perfect place to have a holiday that
includes plenty of opportunities for
outdoor cooking. You can even buy
your logs in the site shop.

cloud farm

The Upside A river, a campsite and some cracking countryside. And some ponies.

The Downside It's a popular site, so at times the shower facilities get a bit stretched.

The Facilities There are 4 showers and 7 loos, 2 washing machines, a dryer and also fridge-freezers. There are 2 washing-up sinks. Dogs are permitted onsite, as long as they are under control.

Onsite Fun Pony-trekking is a big draw, with 11,000 acres to explore, and you won't pass a single car (www.doonevalleytrekking.co.uk). Horses and ponies for all abilities cost £20 an hour.

Offsite Fun Minehead and Woolacombe are good for swimming. Ilfracombe has a good beach and pretty harbour, where you can watch boats. Tunnel Beach (01271 879882; www.tunnelbeaches.co.uk), with 4 tunnels carved in the 1820s leading to a sheltered beach and a tidal-water swimming pool, has plenty of Victorian charm. There are 65 acres of beautiful gardens to explore at Rosemoor (01805 624067; www.rhs.co.uk). The Gnome Reserve (01409 241435; www.gnomereserve.co.uk) is quirky with a pretty wild-flower garden. The wildlife park at Combe Martin (01271 882486; www.dinosaur-park. co.uk) is good for an afternoon out, with wild animals, botanical gardens, brass-rubbing emporium and dinosaur park. Tapeley Park and Gardens (01271 860897/860370; www.tapeleypark. com) is an exceptional sustainable stately home, with a Victorian walled kitchen garden, permaculture garden and straw-bale demonstrations.

If it Rains The Milky Way Adventure Park (01237 431255; www.themilkyway.co.uk) boasts not only Devon's largest roller-coaster, but also a birds-of-prey centre with an indoor falconry area,

'toddler town' and 'fantasy farm', as well as other delights to keep younger children amused. The Mill Adventure Centre (01769 579600; www. milladventure.co.uk) has an indoor climbing wall, as well as outdoor climbing if the weather perks up. You could take the West Somerset Railway (01643 704996; www.west-somerset-railway.co.uk) for a picturesque 20-mile trip from Bishops Lydeard to Minehead, with some tasty snacks like home-baked cakes and local apple juice (and cider) available on board. Tunnel Beach also has an indoor play area with scramble nets and ball pits if you're in Ilfracombe.

Food & Drink There's a small shop onsite for provisions, camping accessories and logs. There's also a good tea shop with excellent cakes and huge scones. You can even get breakfast there. Lynton farmer's market, on the first Saturday of the month, is good for home-baked bread. The best local pub is the Stag Hunter Hotel (01589 741222; www. staghunters.com); the food's pretty standard, but it's a fine place for lunch with kids. Go to Lynmouth for fish and chips, and if you are near Gnome World it's worth dropping in for their home-made snacks.

Nanny State Alert The river is delightful, but dangerous for small children.

Getting There From the A39 Porlock to Lynton Road, take the road to Doone Valley, which is signposted. At Oare Church turn right for Cloud Farm and you will come to the site.

Open All year.

The Damage Low season £5.50 per adult per night, £4 per child. High season £7.50 and £5.50. This site's not to be confused with nearby Doone Valley Campsite.

Cloud Farm, Oare, Nr Brendon, Lynton, Devon EX35 6NU

| t 01598 741234 | w www.doonevalleyholidays.co.uk | **10** on the map |

westermill farm

Stick a pin randomly right into the middle of
a map of Exmoor National Park, and you are
quite likely to spear Westermill Farm. It's a perfect gem,
with creamy rolling hills on all sides.

The River Exe runs beside the camping fields, and Aberdeen Angus cattle and Suffolk sheep graze on the land near by.

The Edwards have farmed here since 1938, and Oliver and Jill run the site from an office lined with an impressive display of rosettes overlooking the farmyard, where chickens scratch around and pigs snooze peacefully in boxes.

If you're a dedicated rider, this is the perfect place to bring your horse on holiday, as cosy stabling is provided for four-legged friends. There aren't any designated play areas at Westermill, but this doesn't mean that it isn't a brilliant family campsite. Far from it. Children can really get stuck in and pretend they're Huckleberry Finn: the river is part of the considerable appeal of the site. They can have a go at dam-making, paddling and swimming and it's a good location for a spot of fishing.

In the evening the furthest field is scattered with families in front of their campfires, but by lights-out time the site is usually pretty quiet: there's no mobile reception and a no-radio policy, so peace and tranquillity reign supreme.

westermill farm

The Upside Rope swings and dam-making keep children happy indefinitely.

The Downside The midges are quite bad on warm, damp evenings.

The Facilities There are 4 camping fields. Pitches are unmarked, with space for approximately 60 tents. The furthest field has campfires and is popular with large groups. There are 2 separate wash-blocks with toilets and showers; solar-powered hot water is boosted with gas. There's a recycling point on this low-impact site. Each field has a fresh-water tap. There's a washing machine (£2), tumble-dryer and sinks. Well-behaved dogs are welcome. BBQs are allowed as long as they are not on the grass.

Onsite Fun Farm animals are a real attraction. As well as the usual suspects there are tortoises and guinea pigs, and usually some chickens and cockerels scratching around. The emphasis is on a working farm: you can bring your own horse on hols, too, as stabling is available. You can go fishing in the river and if you're lucky you'll catch a trout.

Offsite Fun In the middle of Exmoor, Westermill is only 6 miles away from the coast at Porlock; a great walking beach. Woolacombe has a long stretch of beach with fine open sand and excellent rock pools. Quince Honey Farm (01769 572401; www. quincehoney.co.uk) has a fascinating display of open hives. There are some lovely gardens nearby, including Hartland Abbey (01237 441264; www. hartlandabbey.com) – the bluebells in April are gorgeous. Clovelly Court (01237 431781; www. clovelly.co.uk) is a beautiful place for a walk.

If it Rains Watermouth Castle (01271 867474) is an impressive castle sitting just above the sea outside Ilfracombe. There are dungeons, an adventure park and a labyrinth. For a bit of vintage fun, the indoor fairground rides and vehicles at Dingles are worth a visit (01566 783425; www. fairground-heritage.org.uk). The Big Sheep (01237 472366; www.thebigsheep.co.uk) has an indoor playground, and Arlington Court (01271 850296) has a display of exotic treasures.

Food & Drink A shop in the yard sells provisions, including meat. Best local pubs are the Crown Hotel in Exford (01643 831554/5; www. crownhotelexmoor.co.uk) and the Rest and Be Thankful at Wheddon Cross (01643 841222; www. restandbethankful.co.uk), which has good food. The food at the White Horse in Exford (01643 831229; www.exmoor-whitehorse.co.uk) is cheap and cheerful. There's a farmer's market at Minehead on a Friday and a Women's Institute market at South Molton on a Thursday: make a trip to stock up on cakes and jam, and pay a visit to the excellent cheese stand.

Nanny State Alert An unfenced river runs through the site.

Getting There From Exford take the road to Porlock by the Crown Hotel. After a short distance fork left. Continue along this road. You will pass another campsite, but ignore it. There's a sign for Westermill on a tree.

Public Transport Limited. Train to Tiverton, then hop on the 398 bus towards Minehead. The bus stops at Exford, and the site is a 20–30-minute walk from there. In summer, the Exmoor Explorer open-top bus (number 400) travels from Minehead to Exford.

Open Easter–Nov.

The Damage £4.50–5 adult, £2.50–3 child, depending on the season.

Westermill Farm Holidays, Exford, Exmoor, Nr Minehead, Somerset TA24 7NJ

| t 01643 831238 | w www.westermill.com | on the map |

rocks east

A cave, a moss-covered dell, complete with
grotto and woodman on the edge of the 100-acre
forest. All you Enid Blyton fans will be ecstatic to finally
find the enchanted wood incarnate and, possibly,
a magic faraway tree as well.

Most campers return to Rocks East for two reasons: the golden opportunity to sit around an open fire and to have the run of 100 acres of ancient woodland. And wondrous woodland it is, too.

Rocks East has a very distinct culture. On one level it is very much a traditional, basic campsite. It does accept caravans, but canvas is king. All campers can roam free in the forest and the useful illustrated information boards educating novices about flora and fauna are a great resource for adults and kids alike. But this is juxtaposed with what can only be described as bizarre. In the midst of this natural beauty is a teddy-bear trail with garish garden-gnome-type sculptures leering out of the undergrowth. You may be forgiven for thinking you're stuck in some strange land at the top of Enid Blyton's 'magic faraway tree'.

There are no serried ranks as to where you pitch your tent. You can choose your spot, which creates a chilled vibe. Back in the wood, you may be forgiven for thinking that you've checked into a full-on adventure weekend. Don't panic, as the outdoor amphitheatre is sometimes used by outward-bound-type groups. Although if you wanted to stage your own version of *A Midsummer Night's Dream* no one would mind at all.

rocks east

The Upside Traditional camping with open fires. 100 acres of woodland to explore.

The Downside Being an educational trust, it's very popular with groups, especially at weekends, so it's advisable to book. No cycling allowed in the woodland or on the campsite.

The Facilities Two fields at the edge of the forest, sheltered by trees. Log-cabin camp HQ sits in the middle, providing very basic, but clean, facilities. This translates as 1 dishwashing sink plus 1 warm shower, 2 loos and 2 hand basins for ladies, with free hot water; the same for gents. So be prepared for a wait. A twee shop provides basic provisions, such as drinks and sweets, watched over by a dusty selection of woodland taxidermy. There's firewood for sale by the treeload, as well as a selection of hand-whittled wooden items, from walking sticks to bird houses.

Onsite Fun Chilling by an open campfire while the kids roam free. Enjoying everything the forest has to offer, from the badger's hide to a serene nature walk, or even a surreal encounter with carved wooden animals on the Sculpture Trail.

Offsite Fun Cycling or wandering around the country lanes in this area of outstanding natural beauty. If you're cycling, the nearby villages of Marshfield, Colerne and Ford are all good destinations for those not requiring Tour de France-esque distances.

If it Rains Bath is only 20 minutes away, with the Roman Baths, the Royal Victoria Park, and the award-winning young people's Egg Theatre (www.visitbath.co.uk).

Food & Drink The Fox and Hounds at Colerne (01225 744847) is within cycling and walking distance and offers decent children's meals (food from the adult menu, but at smaller prices – we like!). The White Hart at Ford (01249 782213) has the bonus of a riverside setting and does a mean Sunday roast. For lovely local shops that sell local produce for local people (oh, and to a few tourists, too) pop into Marshfield, about 5 minutes' drive away. The Marshfield Central Stores (01225 891260) have a divine deli selling fresh bread and cakes from the Marshfield bakery and Marshfield ice cream – all made in, yep you've guessed it…But if supermarkets are more your bag, there's a Sainsbury's in Chippenham, about 6 miles away.

Nanny State Alert The eerie taxidermy room may cause nightmares.

Getting There Leave the M4 at junction 18 and head towards Bath on the A46. At Pennsylvania roundabout, turn left towards Chippenham on the A420. From the A420 take a right turn into Marshfield and then right again along St Martin's Lane. Follow signs for Ashwicke and Colerne. Continue out of Marshfield, for about 3 miles. The entrance is on the right, clearly marked 'Rocks East Woodland'.

Public Transport Either take the train to Chippenham, then a taxi to the site, or the train to Bath Spa, then the Badgerline bus number 228 from Bath to Hunters Hall. From there it is a 300-metre walk to the site. Call 01225 464446 for a timetable. There is no Sunday service.

Open All year. The word on the campsite is that a blanket of snow in the forest is a magical experience.

The Damage Prices vary according to tent size. High season averages out at about £20 per unit (up to 2 adults and 2 children). Extra charges for awnings, gazebos and additional people. If your family fancies a basic yurt, there's one available for £30 a night.

Rocks East Woodland, Ashwicke, Nr Bath SN14 8AP

| t 01225 852518 | w www.rockseast.org.uk | on the map |

eweleaze farm

A private beach on Dorset's Jurassic Coast
is just for starters; locally sourced organic produce
is the main course, with marshmallows melted over
a roaring campfire for pud. All digested with stunning
sea views. Yum!

The setting at Eweleaze Farm is superb, with panoramic sea views from much of its expansive 80 acres, but it's the refreshing outlook of the proprietor that really makes this place special. It's a laid-back approach that allows campers to enjoy the true freedom of camping – to roam free and choose a pitch anywhere across seven green fields, to forage for firewood (in the designated areas) and build a roaring blaze or to haul straw bales from the barn and plonk them in front of the fire for authentic countryside seating.

This anti-Nanny-State style is a winner with families, who gather here in August, often forming little nylon communes of two or three family groups. For kids, it's down to the beach for swimming, paddling, snorkelling or sandcastling, or perhaps a game of cricket in all this lovely space.

For parents, the backdrop of the Jurassic Coast may be enough entertainment, although the South West Coast Path runs adjacent to the site and is a worthwhile excursion if you can drag yourself away from the campsite.

Eweleaze Farm's greatest asset is undoubtedly the space – not just the physical kind, but the head space too – to relax, to chill and to be a family.

eweleaze farm

The Upside Loads of space, great views, a private beach and campfires. Cracking.

The Downside It's only open during August; advance booking essential.

The Facilities Unmarked pitches are spread over 7 fields; it's agricultural land for 11 months of the year, so don't expect flat, pristine camping pitches. 11 showers in total, including 4 outdoor solar-powered showers. This isn't enough at peak times, but there are plans to increase to 17. Compost toilets or modern toilets in each field; straw bales available for campfire seating; firewood available; the farm shop (8am–8pm) sells organic meat (some frozen), vegetables and other essentials; a wood-fired pizza van (midday–8pm) is a popular option. There are plans to make some of the camping fields car-free, so allow time to ferry equipment to your pitch. Amplified music is prohibited, except on Saturday nights, when it must be off by 11pm.

Onsite Fun Paddling and swimming at the beach, snorkelling in the rock pools, feeding the chickens, scoffing tasty pizza and building a fire.

Offsite Fun The South West Coast Path follows this stunning coastline in both directions from the campsite; an easy 40-minute family walk eastwards takes you to the Smugglers Inn (see Food & Drink). Nearby Weymouth is a great spot for sailing; courses for adults and kids aged 5 upwards are available (£150–165; 0845 3373214; www.lasersailing.com) or you can hire a boat if you're already qualified. For animal action, Monkey World (see p82) is very hard to beat.

If it Rains It's only 5 miles to Dorchester, where there's heaps on offer to keep kids amused. Pick of the crop is the Dinosaur Museum (Icen Way, Dorchester; 01305 269 880;

www.thedinosaurmuseum.com; 9.30am–5.30pm daily) featuring life-size dinos and lots of hands-on exhibits specifically designed for little ones. Other worthwhile museums in town include those devoted to teddy bears, Terracotta Warriors and even Tutankhamun. For more information, visit www.westdorset.com or the Tourist Information Office (Antelope Walk, Dorchester; 01305 267992).

Food & Drink The family-friendly Smugglers Inn (01305 833125) in Osmington is less than 2 miles along the coast path, a view-tastic 40-minute-walk (see p82). For a sunset beer, seek out the terrace of the Cove House Inn (01305 820895; www.thecovehouseinn.co.uk) on Chesil Beach at Portland. It's not exactly Café del Mar, but this no-frills locals' pub, right on the beach, is a good spot to catch the last of the day's rays. Limited organic farm foods are available at the onsite shop.

Nanny State Alert The campsite is half a mile from the main road, down a farm track, so it's fairly safe for the kids to run around without the fear of being run over. There are no known dangerous currents or other hazards at the beach, but there's no lifeguard, so appropriate supervision is required.

Getting There From the east, take the A35 towards Dorchester, then the B3390 and A353 to Osmington. After the village, look out for a speed-limit sign, and turn left here onto a dirt track to the farm. From the west on the A353, continue through Preston, look out for the speed-limit sign just before Osmington, and turn right down the dirt track.

Open End July–end Aug.

The Damage Weekday rates for adults/children are £6/£3, rising to £12/£6 at weekends.

Eweleaze Farm, Osmington Hill, Osmington, Dorset DT3 6ED

| t | 01305 833690 | w | www.eweleaze.co.uk | 13 | on the map |

osmington mills

Pristine, perfect Osmington Mills is part holiday park, part *Cool Camping*. The onsite swimming pool, horse-riding and clubhouse make for an easy family break and you can't see a single static from the tent pitches. Just a big, blue sea.

Dorset's cliff-and-beach coast has all the credentials for that perfect summer holiday. If the sun's shining, everyone's out paddling, playing and rock-pooling. If it rains, the region is well prepared, with aquariums and oceanariums.

With demanding tourists descending here in ever-greater numbers, it's no surprise that many of the campsites have progressed up the evolutionary chain. One such place is Osmington Mills, which once must have started life as a scrawny, scruffy field and has now developed into a highly polished, lovingly manicured camping ground with plenty of awards and accolades to prove it.

Gradual, imperceptible, changes have occurred over the years. Apart from the grass, the amenities have been upgraded and expanded. The result is a highly evolved operation offering a comfortable, easy, hassle-free family holiday.

If evolutionary theorist Charles Darwin had been a camper, this is where he would have stayed. Such perfection won't suit all *Cool Campers*, but the cracking views and coastal location will. Anyway, those seeking a more rough-and-ready site will be around the corner at Eweleaze Farm (see p77). But for those looking for an easy holiday, Osmington Mills is, as Darwin would say, the natural selection.

osmington mills

The Upside Coastal location, sea views, lots of onsite things to do.

The Downside There's a bit of a holiday-park feel, but thankfully most of the facilities are hidden away with the statics.

The Facilities Although officially one big holiday park, the tent campsite is away from the main site. In the tent field itself are 2 pristine amenities blocks (1 with disabled facilities), a laundry room (£3 per wash) and a small shop during high season. A stepped path leads through the trees to the main reception, where a bigger shop stocks groceries and camping accessories. Next door, the Ranch House bar and clubhouse overlooks the pool and offers limited food. It also has a children's room and dubious live entertainment in summer. No hook-ups.

Onsite Fun A good-sized heated swimming pool and shallower sibling (both open May–Sept) mean the kids won't stay dry for long. There are a few games in the kids' room at the clubhouse. The other main onsite attraction is horse-riding; the stables are near the entrance to the tent site and lessons/rides can be booked at reception (01305 833578). A fishing lake (£8) is well stocked with carp and bream.

Offsite Fun There is a small rocky beach about 200 metres from the site. It's fun for rock-pooling or catching little crabs, but the main beach for swimming is the shingle beach at Ringstead Bay, about 20 minutes' drive. It's also accessible on foot via the buggy-unfriendly coast path (30 minutes). The highly acclaimed Monkey World Ape Rescue Centre (01929 450414; www.monkeyworld.co.uk; open all year) is a 20-minute drive away, near Wareham. The kids can check out rescued primates and monkey around on the climbing frames.

Admission for a family of 4 is £31. For other local attractions, see p78.

If it Rains The Tank Museum at Bovington (01929 405096; www.tankmuseum.org; 10am–5pm daily) is fun and informative for kids. They can explore the vast collection of tanks before hitting the shop. There's a café and restaurant with children's menu, as well as a play area outside if the rain subsides. Family tickets cost £29.

Food & Drink Although food is available at the onsite clubhouse, there's a better selection 200 metres down the road at the Smuggler's Inn (01305 833125). It's a cute country pub tucked into a dip, with a little stream running through a pleasant garden kitted out with swings and slides. The food is good-value pub fare and includes local seafood specials; kids' portions available. For supplies to take back to camp, Craig's Farm Shop (01305 834591) sells home-produced dairy products.

Nanny State Alert Nothing dangerous to report.

Getting There From the east, take the A35 towards Dorchester, then the B3390 and A353 towards Osmington. On arrival at Osmington, turn left onto Mills Road signposted 'Osmington Mills', then look out for the campsite signs. From the west head along the A353 through Preston and Osmington, turning right onto Mills Road.

Public Transport Take a train to Weymouth, then a bus (X53) to Poole via Osmington village, or the 108 towards Wool via Osmington village. Then it's on foot for the final half mile down Mills Lane to the site.

Open Mid-March–end Oct.

The Damage Family of 4 costs up to £24, depending on season. Gazebos £4; pets £2.

Osmington Mills Campsite, Osmington, Dorset DT3 6HB

| t 01305 832311 | w www.osmington-mills-holidays.co.uk | 14 on the map |

woodyhyde

A huge site with not-so-friendly staff and makeshift facilities shouldn't really be appearing in this book, should it? We didn't think so either. But the kids just loved running around in all that space. And riding the steam train. Kids, eh?

Don't expect a warm welcome at Woodyhyde. An indifference verging on comedy greeted our arrival, but after failing to get a reaction from Grumpy Man Behind the Counter, we set off to explore the site more thoroughly.

The campsite lies across three fields – a small field adjacent to the Swanage Steam Railway line, a spacious medium field, where you'll also find the main facilities block, and a large field with acres of room and broad, countryside views. Wide-open spaces here are just crying out for rowdy ball games or a few flicks of a frisbee. Unmissable kiddy bliss.

The leafy countryside vista is the perfect backdrop for some early-morning yoga, but don't be alarmed if your meditation is interrupted with a sudden woosh and parp – that'll be the Swanage Steam Railway. The old engines whistle and wheeze past the site between Swanage and Corfe Castle. It's just a pity it doesn't stop right here – the nearest station is at Harman's Cross, 10 minutes' walk away.

Yes, the facilities are a bit rubbish, Mr Grumpy has serious issues and the train runs till eleven at night, but just trust us. You'll like it here. And even if you don't, the kids will. And that's all that matters. Isn't it?

woodyhyde

The Upside Room to move, room to breathe, room to play.

The Downside There is some very minor road noise (although the site is far enough from the road to be safe for the kids). The steam train chugs right past, but you'd have to be pretty uptight to get annoyed by it.

The Facilities Around 150 unmarked pitches on 3 fields across 13 acres, plus a handful of pitches with hook-up. Dogs are allowed in 2 fields; the large field is dog-free. The shower block has seen better days, but is functional if draughty, with 4 showers each for men and women (not really enough for peak times), plus ample loos and basins. No baby-changing facilities or family room. There is a separate washing-up sink outside, identified by the queue after meals. A small shop at reception is open mornings and evenings selling camping essentials plus basics like bread, milk, eggs and ice creams. They also offer icepack re-freezing and calor-gas bottle exchange. Grumpiness is free of charge.

Onsite Fun The large field is the focal point for kids to get together and make friends, and there's usually an impromptu game of football, frisbee or chase going on in all that lovely space. Waving at the steam train and choosing which ice cream to have are other favourite pastimes.

Offsite Fun The long, sandy blue-flag beach at Studland Bay is just 10 minutes' drive from Woodyhyde, and the entire Jurassic Coast, including the lovely Lulworth Cove and the famous Durdle Door rocks, are within easy reach. The ruins of Corfe Castle are in the nearby village of the same name, though cream teas in town may be even more popular. Putlake Farm (01929 422917; www.putlakeadventurefarm.com) at Langton Matravers, offers interactive animal adventures including bottle-feeding lambs and goats. There's also an indoor soft-play zone, outdoor play area and café. Family tickets are £18.50.

If it Rains Hop on the steam train for a ride along the picturesque Swanage Railway through the Isle of Purbeck (01929 425800; www.swanagerailway.co.uk) or further afield, there's both Monkey World and Bovington Tank Museum (for both see p82).

Food & Drink Dorset cream teas are available everywhere, including the particularly welcoming National Trust Tea Room in Corfe Castle. Alternatively, take a walk over Ballard Down, passing Old Harry Rocks and winding up at the bottom of Studland village at the award-winning Bankes Arms Country Inn (01929 450225; www.bankesarms.com). They serve bar snacks and meals of fresh local produce, and a range of ales from small independent breweries, including their own microbrewery.

Nanny State Alert The campsite is set well away from the road and the railway line isn't accessible, so all good and nothing to worry about.

Getting There From the village of Corfe Castle, take the A351 towards Swanage. A mile outside Corfe, look out for the 'Woodyhyde' sign and turning on the right, then follow the track under the bridge and into the campsite.

Public Transport Take the train to Wareham, then bus 142 (not very regular, unfortunately) to Harmans Cross. The bus will stop at the top of Valley Road, and the campsite is about 350 metres down the track from the main road.

Open Easter–Oct.

The Damage Adults £5, children (under 13) £2.50, a family of 4 £13, hook-up £3. Dogs permitted, caravans aren't.

Woodyhyde Campsite, Valley Road, Corfe Castle, Isle of Purbeck, Swanage, Dorset BH20 5HU

| t | 01929 480274 | w | www.woodyhyde.co.uk | 15 | on the map |

mudeford beach huts

A beach hut on a sand spit that you can actually spend the night in? OK, so it's really a glorified Wendy house, but the kids will be in seventh heaven. 'Oh we do like to be beside the seaside…Oh we do like to be beside the sea….'

Mudeford sand spit is, in fact, a sort of shed shanty town: 365 beach huts (one for every day of the year, maybe?) crammed into quite a small space. These huts were originally intended to be sweet little places to change into your swimsuit or make a cup of tea of an afternoon – and now they're stuffed full of families of overnighters. A peaceful haven this is not, but it's a loveable one all the same.

The huts either overlook the Isle of Wight or Mudeford Harbour so, weather permitting, you're ideally placed for some great sunsets and rises. Only a small number of the huts are for hire and what they offer can vary, so do your research before plumping for a particular one. Some are extremely chic, while others are decidedly shabby, but the variety of colours is fabulous. Younger kids love the Wendy-house experience and you may witness doors and windows being flung open to invite new friends in for (play) food and pots of tea. High-season can be frenetic. The place kicks back at night, with candles glowing in windows to supplement the starlight.

There's a touch of Toytown about the place and while it's not everyone's cone of winkles, for novelty factor it scores an easy 10 out of 10.

mudeford beach huts

The Upside Staying on, and waking up to, the beach. Fresh sea air and sand between your toes.

The Downside Can feel cramped both inside and out during high season. Far more peaceful off-season. No pets.

The Facilities The huts vary in facilities. They sleep 4 on average and some have a tiny mezzanine floor; perfect for squeezing in a couple of kids. Some run on solar power, some on gas, some have no electricity at all. Most have a little galley kitchen, with some sort of cooker – and some even have a TV. Water is available from standpipes along the spit and there are 5 loo and shower blocks. You have to bring your own bedding.

Onsite Fun All the fun of the beach: swimming in the sea, building sand-huts and castles, playing hide-and-seek, messing about in boats, nosing at your neighbour's beach hut! Great place to watch the world go by: the Isle of Wight Needles are just across the bay and there are always fishing nets and lobster pots being unloaded on the quay.

Offsite Fun There are several beaches within a drive or boat-ride. Highcliffe is popular with boogie-boarders and you can reach sandy Southborne on the open-top bus. Take a fishing trip (07979 081934). You can even head just across the pond to the Isle of Wight for the day. Take the Wightlink (www.wightlink.co.uk) from Lymington to Yarmouth.

If it Rains Snuggling in the beach hut and peering out through the condensation is fun, as there are always plenty of boats on the water and people to watch. Bournemouth Oceanarium (01202 311993) and the American-style Tower Park (01202 723671), with swimming, bowling and a cinema, in Poole are both about 20 minutes' drive.

Food & Drink The laid-back Beach House Café (01202 423474) is sand-spit central – the hub of the community. Hang out on the sheltered terrace overlooking the marina and enjoy a huge variety of modern British grub, including a children's menu. It also offers an amazingly well-stocked kiosk selling cereal, booze, toiletries, plus anything else that you might have forgotten. For a change of scenery, the Haven Café (01425 272609) on Mudeford Quay offers lattés, teas and standard tourist stuff. Fish fanatics will appreciate the stall on the quay. Buy locally caught turbot, whiting and skate in season to frazzle on the BBQ later, or some fresh snacks to nibble on there and then – polystyrene cup, plastic fork – you know the drill. For Sainsbury's or Waitrose drive to Christchurch.

Nanny State Alert The spit is on the mouth of a fairly sheltered estuary and the open sea is only seconds away, so non-swimmers be aware.

Getting There From Mudeford Quay a boat ferries to and from the sand spit about every 15 minutes, taking 3 minutes and costing about £4 for an average family. Parking is extra. Younger kids prefer the Noddy train option. Park up at Hengistbury Head, paying £15 a day for this privilege, then hop on the brightly coloured train (01202 425517), which deposits you near the beach huts about every quarter of an hour.

Public Transport The nearest train station is Christchurch, then take a taxi to Mudeford Quay to pick up the boat, or to Hengistbury Head to pick up the Noddy train.

Open Early March–end Oct.

The Damage Up to £450 per week for 4 people.

Mudeford Beach Huts, The Spit, Mudeford, Dorset BH23 9ND

t 01202 315437   w www.beach-huts.com   16 on the map

campfire cooking

Cooking over a campfire is one
of the greatest joys of camping.

Campfire cooking with children is great, but it creates its own special challenges. You might have fond dreams of sourcing some locally caught fish to chef up with a bit of lemon and garlic, but it's quite likely that your children will be clamouring for good old burgers and marshmallows – again. If you're not careful you can spend an entire holiday eating Pringles for breakfast, Kit Kats for lunch and a portion of chips, if you're lucky, for supper.

Of course, that's also part of the fun of camping: it skewers domestic routine, which is precisely why children love it so very, very much. What follows is by no means a definitive list of the kind of food you might want to cook with kids while camping (no, if you want that, then beg, borrow or steal a copy of the *Cool Camping Cookbook* for some proper tasty, grown-up friendly fare.)

Instead, the following recipes are guaranteed to bring great big smiles to your children's faces, even in the most inclement weather conditions. Forget all about the calories and the fact that you haven't clapped eyes on your toothbrush for the past week. That doesn't matter. Seeing your children having a great time is actually what it's all in aid of.

garlicky herb bread

Cream 150g of butter until it's nice and soft. Chop up a handful of fresh herbs. Parsley and chives are good choices, but at a push you could use tarragon or coriander instead. Add the herbs and two crushed cloves of garlic to the butter and mix it all together thoroughly. Add salt and pepper, too, if you like. Prepare thick slices of bread by toasting them on a grill over your fire or dry-frying them in a pan. When one side is toasted, spread with a generous knife-full of your butter mixture and return to the grill or pan so that the butter melts through.

orange eggs

Slice the top off an orange, putting the 'lid' on one side, and then carefully scoop out the flesh, while keeping the skin intact. If you have made any holes in the skin, plug them up with a bit of pith. Put a dab of butter inside each orange, and a pinch of salt and pepper, if you like. Carefully crack an egg into each orange, replace the 'lid', then wrap the whole thing in tin foil. Put the parcels onto some glowing coals in your fire. Allow them to cook for about 10–15 minutes before unwrapping them to eat. You can also use this method for other recipes.

campfire baked apples

Cut the top off a large cooking apple, then make an incision into the centre of the apple and remove and discard as much core as you can – down to about halfway is fine. Mix a small handful of raisins with some brown sugar, cinnamon and nutmeg, if you have it. You can even chop up some pieces of ginger very finely, or add a pinch of powdered ginger, but remember that younger children sometimes find fresh ginger a bit too hot. Put a blob of butter into the hole where the core was, then stuff the rest of it with the spicy raisin mix. Blackberries (or any berries you happen to have) can also work well as a stuffing mix. Put another blob of butter on the top, then wrap the stuffed apple in foil and cook on the fire for about 20 minutes.

chocolate banana treats

Carefully slice a banana open along one long side, leaving the two ends sealed. Break up some milk or plain chocolate (Dairy Milk works really well, as does flaked Flake and ripped Ripple). Make small incisions along the centre of the banana and wedge a bit of chocolate inside each incision. Push the remaining pieces of chocolate inside the skin of the banana, then wrap the whole lot in tin foil. Put the parcels onto the fire for 5–10 minutes, depending on the heat of your coals. When you unwrap your banana it should be soft and gooey, and the chocolate melted into a delicious mess.

frankfurter sausage rolls

Add a pinch of salt to 600g of self-raising flour and mix with enough water to form a basic dough. It shouldn't be too wet, but if it is just add a bit more flour. Knead until smooth, then leave to chill out for a bit while you go and find some long, greenish sticks. Scrape the loose skin or bark from the sticks then spear thick Frankfurter sausages onto the end of each stick and push three-quarters of the way down. Roll out sections of dough so that they are relatively thin, then wrap them carefully around your 'dogs'. Cook the dough over some glowing coals. Don't try and cook over flames as the dogs will just burn. When the dough is cooked through, your dogs should be nice and sizzling, too. Slather with ketchup and mustard and eat immediately.

campfire popcorn

Make some roomy tin-foil envelopes, allowing for the fact that the corn is going to expand quite a bit and then pop. Pour a handful of popping corn into each envelope, with a bit of olive oil or some butter. Seal the corn loosely into the envelopes. Put them over the coals or on a grill, turning them over every now and again until the corn stops popping. Using oven gloves or an improvised pot-holder, because the parcels are going to be hot, take them out of the fire and rip them open. Add salt and butter, or any variation of sugar, chocolate powder, golden syrup, honey…delicious!

white horse gypsy caravan

Three days in an original bow-top gypsy caravan,
with a real-live horse to pull it? Clip-clopping through
the picture-perfect Pewsey Vale, life on the open road
doesn't get much better than this.

When you first clamber up the wooden steps and through the door of this traditional vardo, you'll be amazed at how tiny it is. It seems sacrilegious to mess it all up with your family trappings, which look so garish against the delicate hand-painted wood and dainty gingham curtains. While there's no denying it's a squeeze, stow things away and suddenly you'll find that you're in the Tardis.

Getting your trusty steed tacked up, ready for the road, is not as speedy as a car's mirror-signal-manoeuvre, but hearing the creak of the wooden wheels, the clop of the horse's hooves, you'll soon be rocking gently into chillsville.

Your three days are spent plodding through White Horse, stone and crop-circle country, so the place has a special aura. This manifests most strongly at night, especially when you're star-gazing, camped in an open field with a stream trickling near by. You're provided with a real-live groom, who is as hands-on, or -off, as you want, but appears like a lucky charm within minutes of any call for assistance.

Frankly, the only setback could come at the end of your holiday, if your kids decide that actually they would quite like to live in a gypsy caravan all the time, pleeease.

white horse gypsy caravan

The Upside Life on the open road, great overnight camping spots. Freedom.

The Downside The only horse-drawn gypsy caravan in England, so advance booking is a must.

The Facilities The pull-out bed at the back of the caravan sleeps 2 adults (though traditionally this would have slept 2 adults plus the kids). There's room on the floor for a mattress for small ones – or you can take a tent along for them. A vast array of cosy bedding is stashed away. There's a 2-ring gas stove for basic cooking and kettle-boiling, as well as a small electric light. Beneath the caravan is all you need for a BBQ, from charcoal to pans fit for purpose. The service is outstanding, as a cool bag is provided and your groom will drop off newly frozen ice blocks – twice a day if necessary. Your horse is also provided with a bucket, so don't forget to give Tom or Molly plenty of water. All you need to bring, apart from your sense of adventure, is towels, snacks and breakfast plus wet-weather clothes and wellies. If you're wondering about ablutions – you have access to a bathroom at 'base camp' on the first and last night and there's a portaloo awaiting you in the field on night 2. And for other times of day, if you're not near a pub, bushes abound.

Onsite Fun Plodding along the open road in your own house-on-wheels, with your horse doing all the hard graft. Taking it in turns to hold the reins. Waving to passers-by. Admiring pretty thatched cottages. Having a go at bareback-riding in the field at one of the stops, with the groom's approval.

Offsite Fun The itinerary is set in stone, so that you and the horse can get to certain points at specific times for rest, relaxation or running around – especially the predestined overnight camping spot. The ancient stone circle of Avebury (01672 539250; www.nationaltrust.org.uk) is in the vicinity, so some families visit it before or after their 'life on the open road' experience.

If it Rains Put on your waterproofs and relish the fresh air and raindrops on your face. Pit stops abound, including pubs, for opportunities to shelter.

Food & Drink The itinerary is based around family-friendly pubs with good grub, all in beautiful country settings. You'll visit the Barge Inn at Honeystreet (01672 851705; www.the-barge-inn.com), which is a 10-minute walk from base camp. The Millstream at Marden (01380 848308; www.the-millstream.co.uk) has a separate kids' corner, with books and games; especially popular if you've been holed up due to rain. Then there's the Seven Stars at Bottlesford (01672 851325; www.thesevenstars.co.uk) and finally the Woodbridge at North Newnton (01980 630266; www.thewoodbridgeinn.co.uk). There are no shops en route, but if you've forgotten something, just ring Polly or her groom and they'll grab it for you and deliver it at the next pit stop.

Nanny State Alert As you'll be travelling along country lanes with traffic, if you have particularly hyperactive or very young children, this may not be for you. Don't even consider this style of holiday if your kids are scared of horses.

Getting There You start from the base at Alton Priors. Directions on booking.

Public Transport The nearest train station is Pewsey. The owners will pick you up from the station by arrangement, or take a 'Connect2Wiltshire' bus. Book (www.wiltshire.gov.uk) on the Pewsey Vale timetable or by calling 08456 525255.

Open May–Oct.

The Damage £450 for 3 days (starts Friday or Tuesday).

White Horse Gypsy Caravans, Kate's Cottage, Alton Priors, Marlborough, Wiltshire SN8 4JX

| t 01672 851119 | w www.whitehorsegypsycaravans.co.uk | 17 on the map |

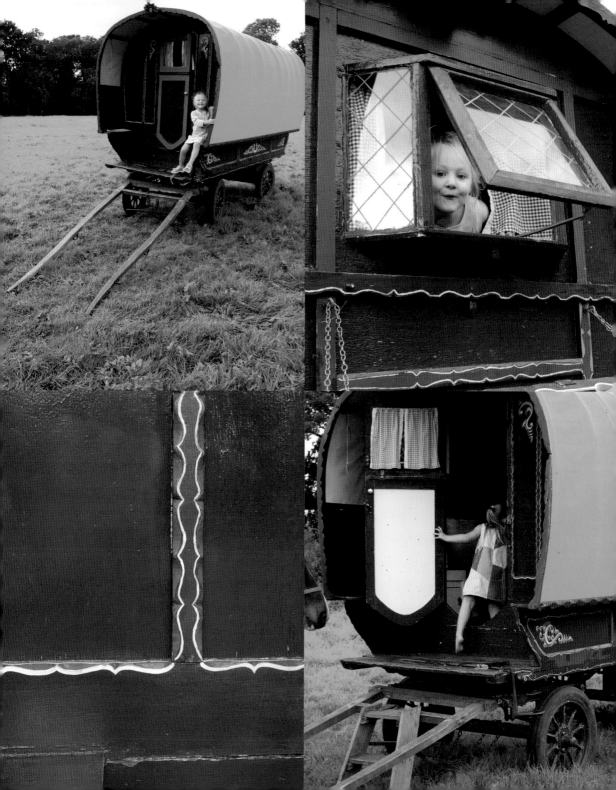

abbey home farm

An eco-camping experience in a green leafy woodland glade on an organic farm. All with a view of lush, green meadows, plus there's an award-winning organic shop and café on your yurt-step. Which, of course, is green in colour.

Abbey Home Farm is not just a beautiful place – it is a living expression of one family's passion. There are quite definitely no food miles here. The organic label is far from being a gimmick or token gesture; this is a farm that has always been at the forefront of the organic farming movement. And it's truly exciting (and delicious, too!) to experience for yourself.

A selection of pitches is scattered around the 1,500 acres of Soil Association-certified organic farm. One option to consider is to bring your own tent and pitch it in the Green Field site, sheltered by the mystical, ancient oaks.

The yurt sites are quite magical and they camouflage perfectly into the surrounding landscape. If the kids do get lost in the greenery of it all, remind them to just look to the skyline and search for the brightly painted totem pole near by. And the signs for the composting loos. And the recycling station. And the sculpture in the tree.

What you and your kids'll get from this camping experience, as well as peace and quiet and a chance to sit in a leafy clearing around a campfire, is a real sense of perspective on life. Organic living isn't just a dream here; it has actually become a reality.

abbey home organic farm

The Upside Eco-camping for real. Cooking on an open fire. Unspoilt natural beauty.

The Downside None to write home about. But the family pooch will have to stay at home, as it's a working farm.

The Facilities The 4-yurt eco-camp (for groups of family and friends) is only a 5-minute walk from the farm shop. There are mattresses to sling on the ground-sheeted floor, wherever the mood takes you, and all the cooking equipment you need. The main yurt has a wood-burner and gas stove, but more fun is cooking on the open fire in the middle of the camp. The single yurt is as well equipped, sleeps up to 5 and is 20 minutes from the café. Composting loos are tucked away in leafy clearings and timed water-squirters let you wash your hands without waste. There's also a green-field campsite by an old oak wood, only 5 minutes by bike to the café. You just turn up during opening hours and grab a pitch. The field has composting loos and a tap. The recycling station is a work of art (literally).

Onsite Fun Running around a totem pole, showering in the wood, cooking on an open fire. No restrictions. Hopping on the back of the tractor-trailer for a farm-tour (when operating). Nipping around the corner to the Farm Shop café for a home-made chocolate brownie.

Offsite Fun You are in Roman-remains territory, so it's mosaics-a-go-go: Chedworth Villa (www.chedworthromanvilla.com) is less than 10 minutes away by car and has some of the best examples. The Corinium Museum in Cirencester (01285 655611) has been recently renovated, with interactive displays and the opportunity to dress up as a Roman soldier. You're also on the edge of the Cotswolds, with Cheltenham and Stow-on-the-Wold within half an hour's drive.

If it Rains Cirencester is only 5 minutes away by car. For creative kids, the Pick a Pot and Paint ceramic studio in Blackjack Street (01285 650405) is worth a punt, while younger ones love the indoor soft play area at MagicLand (01285 885570).

Food & Drink You'll regret bringing any food with you. Buy it here. The farm shop and café produce deliciousness: milk and meat, fruit and veg, cakes and even ready-meals. All organic, of course. There's also a good selection of restaurants in Cirencester. The Hare and Hounds pub at Foss Cross (01285 720288), 4 miles away, has an upmarket dining room, where children's meals aren't your bog-standard deep-fried offerings.

Nanny State Alert The composting loos are very high off the ground, so they're a bit scary and it's a long drop should a little one fall in (though bruises would be the least of their worries).

Getting There From Cirencester, head east for the A417. At the A417 roundabout go straight ahead towards the B4225. After the next roundabout pass the turning for the A429, then take the next left, signposted 'The Organic Farm Shop'.

Public Transport Take the train to Kemble, then a bus to Cirencester (limited service; 01452 425610; www.gloucestershire.gov.uk). From there it is 2 miles to the site. Taxis are available in Cirencester.

Open The yurts are open Easter–Oct. Green Field camping available all year.

The Damage The 4-yurt camp (sleeps up to 18) starts from £550 for a long weekend. The single yurt is £90 for 2 nights. The Green Field campsite is £4 per night per adult, £1 for children.

Abbey Home Farm, Burford Road, Cirencester, Gloucestershire GL7 5HF

t 01285 640441   w www.theorganicfarmshop.co.uk   18 on the map

britchcombe farm

A mysterious white chalk horse gallops across the emerald-green hills of the ancient Ridgeway above Britchcombe Farm. We don't know why it's there, but we know we want to go to see it.

Historians still debate the significance of the wonderful white horses that are to be seen galloping across the south downs of England – you'll see them cut into the soft chalk. Were they religious sites? Fertility symbols? Hunting grounds? Or was making them just Neolithic man's idea of passing the time on a Sunday afternoon? No one knows. But what we do know is that Britchcombe Farm is a magical place to camp, and its proximity to the White Horse must have something to do with it.

The site is owned by the impressive Marcella Seymour, who teaches the uninitiated how to light the perfect campfire (yes, these are allowed here!) and is often up at the crack of dawn taking her sheep to market. When she's not doing that, she's busy either making cream teas or very kindly drying out campers' wet kit in her kitchen. It has to be said, she's nothing less than a national treasure.

If you choose to visit the site on a May morning you're more than likely to bump into a bunch of Maypole-dancing druids. Whatever our ancient cousins were up to here, you won't find much better mystical credentials than that.

britchcombe farm

The Upside Fantastic views across Wiltshire, Berkshire and Oxfordshire beneath the ancient chalk hill of the Ridgeway; lighting a fire is an added bonus.

The Downside Very popular on mystical evenings such as the solstices, so book in advance.

The Facilities Five camping fields of about 20 acres dotted on either side of the road, with 2 family fields. There are a few hook-ups in the caravan field. The 5 showers, 3 toilets and washing-up sinks are beside the farmhouse, but each field has its own portaloo. Although there are no clothes-washing facilities, Marcella has been known to dry out wet kit in her kitchen. There's also a tipi that sleeps 4 people. It has a double mattress and 2 singles, plus blankets, sheepskins and cooking equipment. Bring your own bedding. Fires are allowed onsite, and Marcella delivers logs and paper (£5) at dusk.

Onsite Fun There's nothing specific for children onsite, but it is popular with families, and there's usually an impromptu football match going on in the family field. There are chickens in the farmyard.

Offsite Fun White Horse Hill is just above the site, and the Ridgeway is riddled with hill forts and long barrows. Nearby is Dragon Hill (www. berkshirehistory.com), where St George is supposed to have slain his dragon, and a half-hour walk away is Wayland's Smithy, an impressively spooky Neolithic burial chamber. The little museum of Tom Brown's School (01367 820259; www.museum. uffington.net) in the village is open Saturday afternoons, and at other times for groups. The dreaming spires of Oxford are only 45 minutes away; the Pitt Rivers Museum (01865 270927; www.prm. ox.ac.uk) has totem poles, voodoo dolls and famously grizzly shrunken heads. Back near the site, Farmer Gow's (01793 780555; www.farmergows. co.uk) is popular with younger children. In spring you can feed farm animals, including lambs and piglets.

If it Rains There's a swimming pool in Wantage (01235 760884; www.wantage.com), and a bigger one in Swindon (01793 445401; www.swindon.gov. uk) with slides and wave machine. Didcot Railway Centre (01235 817200; www.didcotrailwaycentre. org.uk) has old engines. Bourton-on-the-Water (www.bourtoninfo.com) has a model village, Birdland (01451 820480; www.birdland.co.uk) and a maze.

Food & Drink Marcella does cream teas on Sundays, spring–Oct. The White Horse at Woolstone (01367 820726; www.whitehorsewoolstone.co.uk) does very good food. If you find yourself hooked on ley lines and other mystical magic, try the Barge Inn at Alton Barnes. The standing stones at Avebury and Silbury Hill are very close, and the pub is a mine of knowledge on crop circles. If you're in Oxford go to the fish stall in the covered market, with live lobsters and crabs in tanks, and sometimes a dead shark on display, too.

Nanny State Alert Watch the road between the farm and the family fields; it's small but cars can speed along it.

Getting There Come through Wantage on the B4507, following a signpost for 'Wayland's Smithy'. Stay on that road for nearly 6 miles and the farm is the first on the left-hand side on a bend.

Public Transport Not really recommended, but you can take a train to Oxford or Didcot Parkway. Regular buses from both stations to Wantage, where you can take a taxi to the site or a bus to Uffington and the site is a mile's walk from there.

Open All year.

The Damage £6 adult, children 5–14 years £3; tipi £40 a night (for tipi hire only call 07974 438566).

Britchcombe Farm, Uffington, Faringdon, Oxfordshire SN7 7QJ

t   01367 820667

19 on the map

swiss farm

If you happen to be in Henley, but want a good reason to avoid the Regatta, here's your excuse. At Swiss Farm you'll find tranquil, landscaped camping at the foot of the Chilterns, complete with lake and swimming pool. Perhaps you could hold your own regatta!

At first glance, Swiss Farm seems worryingly commercial and a little too large-scale to feature in our book. But first impressions can be deceptive, and once you've spied the spacious adventure playground, the outdoor swimming pool and the still waters of the willow-fringed fishing lake, your reservations will soon evaporate.

Just outside the quintessentially English town of Henley-on-Thames, this site is a great place to stay during the festivities of the summer's Royal Regatta, an annual event launched way back in 1839. In those days it was all about the rowing races, watched by moustachioed, straw-boater-wearing Victorian gents, who stood on the river banks clapping genteelly. Nowadays the crowd is quite a bit more raucous and the races seem to play second fiddle to days of riverside fun and frolics in the sun.

At quieter times of the year, Swiss Farm is simply a great place to come and relax by the lake, a base from which to explore Oxfordshire's countryside, hills and interesting towns. And in the evenings it's a place to enjoy family BBQs in the dusky evening glow.

swiss farm

The Upside Full of fun for kids – swimming pool, indoor games, play area, rabbits to chase, lake to fish and loads of space. All an oar's length from regatta-hotspot Henley-on-Thames.

The Downside Caravans. So many caravans. In rows. Luckily they have their designated fields. It can also get pretty crowded and pricey in summer, especially when the Royal Regatta (first week of July) is on.

The Facilities Two large facilities blocks. Free hairdryers and baby-changing cubicles. Laundry, wi-fi and hook-ups all available.

Onsite Fun Kids can splash about in the open-air swimming pool (open June–Sept) as mums and dads relax at the picnic tables with a refreshing drink from the onsite bar. A small playground in a spacious, rabbit-inhabited field, and lake for fishing (£2 per child, £3 per adult for half a day) and duck-feeding provide drier alternatives.

Offsite Fun Odds Farm Park (01628 520188; www.oddsfarm.co.uk; family of 4 approx £30) is a 25-minute drive away, offering a fantastic family day of farmyard fun. There's hands-on bottle-feeding lambs, sheep-shearing and milking demonstrations, mini-golf and go-karting, so there's no room whatsoever for boredom.

If it Rains The River and Rowing Museum (Mill Meadows, Henley-on-Thames; 01491 415600; www.rrm.co.uk; family of 4 £20) may not sound like the funnest thing to do on a wet day, but as Ratty said: 'there is NOTHING, absolutely nothing, half so much worth doing as simply messing about in boats.' This award-winning museum is full of boats, as well as a fantastic *Wind in the Willows* gallery.

Food & Drink Grab some of the fantastic meat available at Gabriel Machin butchers (Market Place; 01491 574377) for a smokin' BBQ back at the site. This quality butcher has been around since 1910 and can boast of supplying meat to the likes of Antony Worrall Thompson, so all you have to do is buy a disposable BBQ from Swiss Farm's reception and ready, steady cook!

Nanny State Alert The lake is easily accessible, so keeping an eye on youngsters is a must. Cars come and go, but should be slow. The pool is fenced off when closed, and the playground is in the middle of a field behind a thick hedge.

Getting There Exit the M4 at Junction 8/9, taking the second exit at the roundabout onto the A404. After 2¾ miles take the Henley-on-Thames exit, which merges onto Henley Road (A4130). Follow this onto Henley Bridge. At the traffic lights go straight on into Hart Street, then turn right onto Bell Street. You'll come across 2 mini roundabouts, go straight over the first, then turn right at the second onto Marlow Road. The campsite is just on the left.

Public Transport Take a train to Henley-on-Thames and a walk through the town onto Marlow Road.

Open March–Oct.

The Damage A pitch without hook-up for a family of 4 (kids aged 5–15) with 1 car costs between £13 (low season) and £20 (peak). Prices during Regatta Week £20–40 per night; booking at least a week in advance is essential. Dogs are only permitted during low season.

Swiss Farm International Touring & Camping, Marlow Road, Henley-on-Thames, Oxon RG9 2HY

t 01491 573419	w www.swissfarmcamping.co.uk	20 on the map

st ives farm

In deepest Sussex lives a bear called Pooh.
He looks funny, eats honey, but what else is there to do?
A game of Pooh Sticks at Pooh Bridge is good,
then a campfire and sing-song in
Hundred Acre Wood.

If there's one kids' character whose appeal transcends generations, it's that lovable bear Winnie the Pooh. Having graduated from story books to TV shows to the movies and Disneyland, Winnie is now a big-time celebrity in a billion-dollar global franchise.

Such big names attract adulation and interest, and just as die-hard fans flock to the zebra crossing on Abbey Road, once traversed by the Beatles, so too do people descend on the significant locations that have featured in the life of this remarkable bear. The epicentre of all this activity is the unassuming Surrey village of Hartfield, home of the Pooh Corner café and the sweetshop where Christopher Robin used to buy his bulls' eyes. In the surrounding countryside are to be found the renowned Hundred Acre Wood, Pooh Bridge (supposedly the birthplace of Pooh Sticks) and St Ives Farm campsite.

Admittedly, the campsite is nothing at all to do with Pooh, but it's perfectly located for all this Pooh-phernalia and is a wonderfully quiet and appealing place. The leafy pitches encircle a fishing lake and the permitted campfires offer the ideal setting to get the family together and read the kids a story. Now, I wonder, what would be a good book...?

st ives farm

The Upside Pooh Sticks by day, Pooh stories by the campfire at night.

The Downside The basic facilities and a noticeable caravan count.

The Facilities A caravan field also containing the shower block is the first field you'll see on arrival. Just beyond is the fishing lake, around which about 20 tents can be pitched. The basic facilities won't be to everyone's taste, but they suit this rustic place; just 7 loos (3 of which are portaloos) and 2 showers.

Onsite Fun Other than making campfires, the only other conventional onsite activity is fishing. The lake is stocked with carp and perch and costs £5/£9 per day for children/adults. Almost onsite is the adjacent tea garden, which serves tasty cream teas and light lunch snacks against an Ashdown Forest backdrop.

Offsite Fun Do as Pooh would do – eat honey, play Pooh Sticks and wander around in the woods. In Hartfield, the old sweetshop where Christopher Robin used to buy bulls' eyes survives to this day, re-named Pooh Corner and now doing a roaring trade in cream teas, pots of honey and general Pooh-phernalia. If you're not too Pooh-ped after all that, then you can go walking with llamas (no, really) at the Ashdown Forest Llama Park (01825 712040; www.llamapark.co.uk) in Forest Row. One llama each is £30; 2 people sharing a llama is £50. Bizarre, but true.

If it Rains Make sure you pack a good board game in preparation for a cosy day holed up at the Hatch Inn (see Food & Drink). There's always Tunbridge Wells' Odeon cinema (Knights Park, Knights Way, Tunbridge Wells; 0871 2244007). There are also some grand homes to explore in the area, including the moated 13th-century Hever Castle (01732 865224; www.hevercastle.co.uk) about 7 miles away in Hever, near Edenbridge and Sir Winston Churchill's family home at Chartwell (01732 868381; www.nationaltrust.org.uk) about 12 miles north of Hartfield on the B2026.

Food & Drink For top-notch food, with an emphasis on locally sourced, seasonal produce, head for the Hatch Inn (01342 822363) at Colemans Hatch. It's a quaint little country pub on the edge of Ashdown Forest, a 50-minute walk, or 10-minute drive, from St Ives Farm and handy for Pooh Sticks Bridge. French and traditional British cuisine feature on a changing, innovative menu, served in a snug restaurant or in the beer garden.

Nanny State Alert The lake is not fenced and there are campfires everywhere. So the kids will love it, but protective parents may not.

Getting There Follow the A22 southbound through South Godstone. Shortly after Brindley Heath, take a left onto the B2029 (Ray Lane) towards Lingfield. The road turns into the B2028 (Race Course Road). Turn right when you reach Dormans Road, which eventually becomes Hollow Lane and then meets the A264. Turn left onto the A264 for 1.4 miles then turn right onto Cansiron Lane, which turns slightly left, becoming Butcherfield Lane. The campsite is a little further on the right and is clearly signed.

Open April–late Oct.

The Damage A family of 4 costs £16 per night, a family of 6 costs £20. Dogs are welcome, and are free to frolic in their very own designated dog-walking area.

St Ives Farm, Butcherfield Lane, Hartfield, East Sussex TN7 4JX

t 01892 770213

21 on the map

wapsbourne manor farm

With smoky campfires, dodgy old rope-swings and free camping for musicians every Friday night, this is not a site for the Nanny-State obsessed. But go with the flow and this rural wonderland is the perfect outdoor adventure playground.

Wapsbourne Manor Farm, or 'Wowo', as it's affectionately known by regular customers, is a rare and beautiful thing – a decent campsite within two hours' drive of London. It's also the least ruled-and-regulated site you could possibly find in this sue-or-be-sued compensation culture. Campfires are allowed, and to facilitate this a firewood delivery man comes around at dusk on his little tractor; camping's equivalent of room service and an evening turn-down all in one.

Children's entertainment is strictly old school: climbing trees, swinging on tyres, rolling around in ditches, making camps in the undergrowth.

In fact, the entire 150-acre site is a huge, natural adventure playground. With no allocated pitches, you can pick a spot on one of the four or five fields. Or is it six or seven? This magical place always seems to have something new to discover; another field hidden behind the thicket, a secret pathway, a yurt nestled among the trees. With the evening air scented with campfire smoke, the soft murmur of sociability and the odd sing-song soundtrack, this wonderful place just oozes back-to-basics appeal.

Leave the rules at home. Let the kids roam free.

wapsbourne manor farm

The Upside A cracking, chilled-out atmosphere and 'to-your-tent' firewood delivery.

The Downside A circle of statics at reception is the only downer, but they're an insignificant feature of this huge site.

The Facilities An undefined number of unmarked pitches across an unconfirmed number of fields. Limited woodland pitches and 2 yurts also available. The main toilets and hot showers are in clean portacabins; there are also 4 composting loos in little sheds in various corners of the site. There are laundry facilities by reception, where they will also charge your phone and re-freeze your icepacks.

Onsite Fun Making camps, hiding in the woods, getting muddy, climbing trees. There is also a kids' room with table tennis and a pool table.

Offsite Fun Go for a wander around the beautiful National Trust landscaped gardens at Sheffield Park (01825 790231), just up the road. Kids can run about, feed the swans and ducks by the lake and enjoy the children's trail. Family admission from £16.50. It's also possible to combine a Bluebell Railway ticket (see If it Rains) with gardens admission. If it's sunny, nip down to Brighton for a day of good ol'-fashioned seaside frolicking.

If it Rains With a station right next door to Wowo, the Bluebell Railway (01825 720825; www.bluebell-railway.co.uk) has a big collection of steam locomotives – perfect for a Thomas the Tank Engine-inspired day out.

Food & Drink Avoid the appalling, overpriced tea rooms at Sheffield Park Gardens at all costs. Instead, head a bit further up the A275 to Trading Boundaries (01825 790200; www.tradingboundaries.com; open 10am–6pm), a delightful café and eclectic furniture and antiques shop. There is also a great farm shop, the Dairy Shop, a bit further up the road on the left. There is no shortage of pubs in the area. The family-friendly Sloop Inn (Scayne's Hill; 01444 831219) is a 40-minute walk from the campsite, through shady woodland and serves up hearty food and local ales. A kids' menu is available and there is a good-sized beer garden. For foodies, there are 2 excellent gastro-pubs; the Michelin-rated Coach and Horses (School Lane, Danehill; 01825 740369; www.coachandhorses.danehill.biz) and the Griffin (Fletching; 01825 722890; www.thegriffininn.co.uk), both less than 10 minutes' drive.

Nanny State Alert If you're concerned about health and safety, best not come here. With campfires, rope swings and lots of mud, there's just too much to worry about.

Getting There From the M25, exit at junction 6 and take the A22, following signs for the 'Bluebell Railway'. Keep going, past the railway on the right and Wapsbourne is the second entrance on the right (look for the strawberry signs). From the south take the A275 north towards the Bluebell Railway/ Sheffield Park. Once you've crossed over the A272 at Chailey the campsite is located 1½ miles ahead on the left.

Public Transport The nearest station is Haywards Heath, from where a taxi costs about £15. Or you could arrive on the Bluebell Railway, but that's only really useful if you happen to live in Kingscote or Horsted Keynes.

Open By the time you read this the site should be open year-round, subject to planning consent. Best call to check.

The Damage Family of 4 costs £24; firewood £5. Dogs are allowed. The yurts cost from £85 a night.

Wowo, Wapsbourne Manor Farm, Sheffield Park, East Sussex TN22 3QT

t 01825 723414	w www.wowo.co.uk	22 on the map

safari britain

This site is like being dropped into the middle of a Bloomsbury-set house party. And, if you want even more glamour, you can take a trip down the road to Glyndebourne for some operatic high culture. But do remember to wear your dressing gown.

It is said that Lydia Lopokova, the eccentric and colourful Russian ballerina of the twenties and thirties, danced naked along the chalk hill behind the site for her husband John Maynard Keynes. She was one of the many Bloomsbury eccentrics who gathered at Charleston. She also went to the opera at Glyndebourne wearing her dressing gown.

Perhaps she set a precedent, because an atmosphere of bohemia pervades this site. Absolutely everything that you want, and probably a lot more besides, is onsite, including pre-erected bell tents and a glorious yurt, which sits in a sunny bowl of the Sussex

Downs, surrounded by 300-year-old oak trees, a chalk track peeling across the fields and the sea the other side.

The kitchen looks like a vintage-style photo shoot; shelves stocked with old French enamel, silver-plated delights, copper cooking pots and a gigantic frying pan big enough to cook a fry-up for the whole site. Children will love the optional activities, including foraging and bow-and-arrow-making, or they could easily spend an afternoon building dens, climbing trees and exploring – miles from the nearest house or road – while you stretch out with the Sunday papers.

safari britain

The Upside You really do not have to take anything. Except possibly booze.

The Downside You might feel you could live here forever, but all good things have to come to an end.

The Facilities The site sleeps a maximum of 16 people in 6 bell tents, each of which has mattresses, linen, duvets and lanterns. There's a gorgeous yurt, furnished like a Moroccan souk with embroidered rugs, skins, sofas, cushions and wood-burning stove. Laundry (includes sheets, duvet and towel) is an extra £10 per head. There's a kitchen, although you can also cook on the huge central fire pit or BBQ; all pots and pans are provided. There's an eco sawdust loo and a shower under a 200-year-old oak tree. Everything is provided.

Onsite Fun In the yurt there are maps, reference books, guitars, board games, kites, bats and balls. You can try plant-foraging for supper, find out how to cook rabbits, squirrels or snails. Or you could learn fire-making or den-building. A falconer brings birds of prey for everyone to see, and you can have a landscape-drawing lesson, study local wildlife or go on a bird-song walk.

Offsite Fun The South Downs National Trail is 5 minutes above the campsite. At the Seven Sisters Country Park the museum has bike and canoe hire. Because this is Bloomsbury country, Charleston (01323 811265; www.charleston.org.uk) is just next door. See the Long Man of Wilmington (a giant figure carved into the Downs' chalk). At Wilmington church try brass-rubbing and admire stained-glass windows of local butterflies. Local swimming places are good; try Tide Mills near Seaford or between the chalk cliffs at Hope Gap.

If it Rains Drusillas Park zoo near Alfriston (01323 874100; www.drusillas.co.uk) has a big playground and train. Five minutes away by car you will find Middle Farm (01323 811411; www.middlefarm. com), which has an 'open farm area', where children can visit animals and see milking in action. There is also an outdoor playground and a hay play barn, a nature trail and picnic area.

Food & Drink Twenty minutes' walk away is the Ram in Firle (01273 858222; www.bushywood. com), and further afield is Rose Cottage, Alciston (01323 870377). The village shop in Firle is good for basics, but Middle Farm Shop has excellent local produce. For grown-ups the cider house is an essential pit stop, on the pretext of buying apple juice for the kids.

Nanny State Alert Ponies sometimes wander up to the camp, even though it is fenced.

Getting There From London, take the M23 south to Brighton and then follow the A27 East past Lewes. Seven miles beyond Lewes, and shortly after the entrance to Charleston (on the right), you'll arrive at the village of Selmeston. Immediately after the Barley Mow pub take the turning right to Bo Peep Lane, signposted 'By Way'. Follow the road for 1 mile until you reach a cluster of buildings on your left. Turn right opposite Bo Peep B&B onto the old chalk coach road. After a short distance, Old Shepherd's Cottage is on the right, followed by an old Sussex barn. Parking is just beyond the barn. The site is about 15 minutes' walk.

Public Transport Take a train to Lewes or Glynde and then taxi to Firle. Rural bus services would probably deliver you after the event.

Open May–end Sept.

The Damage £120 per adult, £60 a child per weekend. £1,450 for exclusive use of the site, with a maximum of 16 people. Book early.

Safari Britain, Old Shepherd's Cottage, Firle, Sussex BN8 6LL

| t | 07818 064456/07780 871996 | w | www.safaribritain.com | 23 | on the map |

cobbs hill farm

Who doesn't love animals? Furry ones, shaggy ones, stinky ones. This cute collection of pet-able lovelies will enthral the kids for simply seconds – before scampering off to the big field to join the beasts of the two-legged, home-counties, variety.

Hip and Hop are lion-head rabbits. They scamper around all day, sniffing and scratching and occasionally saying hello to children. They're furry and cute, and when you're used to rabbits of the standard, domestic, variety, these hairy munchkins are a wonder to behold. They would undoubtedly taste great on a BBQ.

But the animals aren't here to be barbecued, they're here to entertain the kids. Not in a performing-circus kind of way, more in a 'look there's a lion-head rabbit' kind of way. Which is a nice diversion when the kids have started screaming at each other like hyenas. Animals aside, Cobbs Hill Farm is made for kids.

It's safe and well ordered and however many tents are lined up in the camping area in high season, there are always two fields empty and open for playtime.

A decent adventure playground has a ropey climbing thing, a space-shippy roundabout thing and a swinging tyre thing, all made with sturdy wood and good craftsmanship. And those foamy soft-landing areas will help minimise the bruise-count. As for the animals, there are also horses, goats and guinea pigs to get acquainted with. None of which are much good for the BBQ.

cobbs hill farm

The Upside Playgrounds plus animals equals lots of happy kids.

The Downside No views, no campfires, a bit strict; possibly a tad regimented for free-spirited mummies and daddies.

The Facilities Much of the site is reserved for caravans, but the dedicated camping field has level pitches and some hook-ups. A dated but clean and functional toilet and shower block has just 2 showers each for males and females; possibly not enough in peak times, but then demand may be reduced by the annoying coin-operated shower system (20p). There are also 2 family rooms with showers. Hairdryers, shaver points and laundry facilities (£2) are all available. A small shop at reception sells bread, milk, newspapers, camping gas and ice creams. They also charge up batteries and will re-freeze icepacks.

Onsite Fun As well as the animals, the main kids' attraction is the playground; the large, dedicated children's play area often has goals, and other bits and bobs for the kids to use.

Offsite Fun Bexhill (3 miles away) is a quaint, old-fashioned seaside resort with a pebbly beach and a few interesting shops, or for more action and adventure, you could always take the kids sailing (Bexhill Sailing Club; 01424 212906). The historic town of Battle (5 miles away) offers shops, pubs, restaurants, Battle Abbey itself, plus the 1066 Visitor Experience – a family exhibition that tells the story of the Battle of Hastings.

If it Rains Bexhill Leisure Pool (01424 731508) has a wave machine, a long twisty slide and a café to chill out in afterwards. Family swimming admission costs £10. Hastings is only 5 miles away and has a cinema, Smugglers' Adventure Caves (01424 422964) and castle built by none other than William the Conqueror.

Food & Drink There are plenty of family-friendly pubs and restaurants in Battle; go via Catsfield village if you need to stock up on delicious fruit and veg – the farm shop there at Great Park Farm Nursery (01424 772531; www.greatparkfarm.co.uk) offers high-quality produce plus a range of biscuits, cakes, chutneys and preserves. Battle Deli (58 High Street, Battle) has a great selection of tasty breakfast pastries, healthy lunch snacks and cakes. But forget all that healthy stuff, what could be better than fish and chips from a polystyrene tray on Bexhill prom?

Nanny State Alert The adjacent fields may have animals from neighbouring farms, so kids shouldn't stray beyond the obvious campsite boundaries.

Getting There From the A21 towards Hastings, take the A2100 to Battle, then the A271 until you reach a left turn onto the B2204 towards Ninfield. At Ninfield take the A269 southbound. Look out for a left turn onto Watermill Lane. The site is about 1 mile down Watermill Lane on the left. From the south-east take the A259 towards Hastings until you reach the A269 towards Ninfield. Take the A269 past Sidley and look for Watermill Lane on the right.

Open Easter/April–late Oct.

The Damage £13.50–17.50 for family of 4 with car (depending on season and whether you want hook-ups); dogs 50p (please keep on leads). Security gates are closed at 11.30pm.

Cobbs Hill Farm, Watermill Lane, Bexhill, East Sussex TN39 5JA

t 01424 213460   w www.cobbshillfarm.co.uk   24 on the map

cliff house

Cliff-top, woodland site with direct access to the beach. Sounds good? It gets better! It's right bang next door to a bird reserve – so pack your kites, bikes, binoculars and walking boots to make the most of your trip.

If you look at the website before your visit, don't be put off by the emphasis on holiday cottages and caravans. This 30-acre woodland site has lots of prime tent pitches among the trees and on the lawn in front of the house.

If hide-and-seeking in the woods, peddling along the figure-of-eight-shaped path through the site or ball games aren't enough to keep the kids busy, they can always head off to the playground for climbing, swinging and sliding, or to the indoor family games room for table football and pool. Or go and visit the neighbours! The National Trust's Dunwich Heath Coastal Centre and Beach is right next door.

Steps (rather steep ones) take you down to the stony beach at the bottom of the cliff, where you can fly kites, beachcomb or paddle in the sea, or take the short walk along the beach to the Coastal Centre, for porpoise- and seal-spotting in the Seawatch Room.

Also on the doorstep (or should that be tentstep?) is the Minsmere bird reserve, which has hides and nature trails throughout the heath, woodland, beach and dunes, and organises special events all year. You can try your hand at nestbox-building and join in their bird-watching safaris.

cliff house

The Upside Peaceful, woodland site with direct access to the beach, glimpses of the sea through the trees and a playground.

The Downside Campers share the site with touring caravans, statics and holiday lodges. The prices are a little steep on Bank Holiday weekends.

The Facilities There are around 90 marked pitches (40 for tents) spread throughout the woods or on the flat grassy lawn in front of the house. The shower blocks have recently been refurbished, with 3 showers, 4 toilets and 4 washbasins for women, and 3 toilets, 3 showers and 3 washbasins for men in the main block. There are 4 washing-up sinks and a launderette with 2 washing machines and 2 tumble-dryers. The playground has climbing frames, swings, football goals and a slide, and there is also an onsite indoor games room, pub and restaurant. A small shop (selling all the basics) is open all day and during the evenings in high season, and from 8.30am–3pm in low season, as well as evenings if it is busy enough.

Onsite Fun Children love being in the woods, and the site is also good for cycling around. The grassy area in front of the house is perfect for ball games. The playground and games room make meeting other kids easy.

Offsite Fun A 10-minute drive (or hour's stroll) takes you into Walberswick. Here you can do a spot of crabbing (it's the home of the British Open Crabbing Championships) before hopping onto a foot ferry for a short ride over the water, or take a longer boat trip from the harbour. Alternatively walk into Southwold, with its sandy beach, colourful bathing huts and quirky pier with hand-made penny-slot machines. The National Trust's Dunwich Heath Coastal Centre and Beach (01728 648501; www.nationaltrust.org.uk) is next door. The RSPB's Minsmere reserve (01728 648281; www.rspb.org.uk) has hides and nature trails.

If it Rains The site has a family games room with a TV, pool table and table football, but the towns of Southwold and Aldeburgh are both only about 20 minutes' drive away.

Food & Drink The pub/restaurant on the site does pub grub and children's meals, and the National Trust tea room along the beach at the old Coastguard Cottages (01728 648501) has splendid views and boasts the best puds on the Suffolk coast. If fish and chips are more your thing, head for the Flora Tearooms on the beach car park at Dunwich. If you fancy more upmarket pub dining, children are welcome at the Crown in Westleton (01728 648777), which even bakes its own bread.

Nanny State Alert The steps down to the beach are quite steep, so hold on tight to young children.

Getting There Heading north on the A12 from Ipswich, turn right at the sign for Westleton and Dunwich. Carry on to the end of the road and at Westleton turn left. Drive through the village and turn right at the top of the hill towards Dunwich. Continue until you see brown caravan signs and turn right onto Minsmere Road. The campsite is about 1 mile down this road on the left. (Beware: there are two Cliff House campsites, so make sure you are heading for the one at Dunwich rather than Sizewell.)

Open Early March–end Oct.

The Damage A family of 4 in a tent on a standard pitch would pay between £18 and £22.60, depending on the season (£30.40 on popular Bank Holidays). Dogs can come too (£1.70–2.70).

Cliff House Holiday Park, Minsmere Road, Dunwich, Saxmundham, Suffolk IP17 3DQ

| t 01728 648282 | w www.cliffhouseholidays.co.uk | 25 on the map |

clippesby hall

Safe, comfortable, highly organised Clippesby is
the first-time family-campers delight. From the mini-golf
to the swimming pool, from the well-stocked shop to
the family-friendly pub, it's all here, like a posh version
of Butlins. Hi de hi, campers!

The idea of holiday camps is inherently a very good one. Lots of activities for the kids, good-value food, comfortable accommodation and, most importantly, a bar for the grown-ups. But somehow, when you put these elements together, the result can be quite horrible.

But it's all in the execution, and what the guys at Clippesby have achieved is to craft an exceptionally family-friendly, children-entertaining site without resorting to the tacky bright-light arcade-culture of the plastic parks. Instead, it's traditional, wholesome activities you'll find here, like crazy golf, swimming and tennis on real grass courts.

It's a largish site and does get busy during peak times, but there are half a dozen different camping areas, so it never feels as if you're all lined up like old-men's legs in a knobbly knees contest.

While Clippesby isn't the quietest, peaceful-est *Cool Camping* campsite, it is possibly the family-est. With its flat, sheltered, spacious pitches, it's the easiest, too. What's more, it's all packaged in a neat, refined, country-estate garden setting. *Brideshead Revisited* meets Maplin's, if you like, although it's quite definitely more Emma Thompson than Ruth Madoc.

clippesby hall

The Upside Everything you'll need for the family, except the Redcoats.

The Downside It can get busy (and a bit noisy) during peak season.

The Facilities As well as the kids' facilities (see Onsite Fun, below) there is a handy café, a small shop and a relaxed family pub with outdoor terrace, serving good-value family meals. Clean and plentiful toilets and showers are found in subtle wood-clad structures; family bathrooms are available.

Onsite Fun Kids will be in their element here; a small swimming pool, grass tennis courts, kids' play areas, cycle-hire centre, crazy golf, volleyball and football are all available.

Offsite Fun Explore the waterways of the Norfolk Broads; the village of Potter Heigham, 4 miles north of Clippesby, has several boatyards offering a variety of piloted or self-drive boats. Try Broads Tours (01692 670711; www.broads.co.uk) at Herbet Woods boatyard for piloted pleasure trips complete with running commentary. For animal fun, head to nearby Thrigby Hall Wildlife Gardens (Filby, Great Yarmouth; 01493 369477; www.thrigby.plus.com), where crocodiles lurk, tigers crouch and primates monkey around in the forest house. Admission for a family of 4 costs £32. If they'd rather catch animals than look at them, then take the kids fish-hunting with a professional local angler (01603 714352).

If it Rains The tacky, mildly depressing seaside resort of Great Yarmouth is only 10 miles away, and while it won't be winning any prizes for prettiness or tourist innovation, it does have endless amusement arcades and a pier. There is a Sea Life Centre (01493 330631) there, too, but the Seal Sanctuary (01485 533576; www.sealsanctuary.co.uk) up in Hunstanton is much more entertaining, though a bit of a trek away.

Food & Drink The onsite shop sells local and Fairtrade produce, and you can get local ales and ciders at the onsite pub, the Muskett Arms. Morton's Farm (01603 712320) in North Burlingham has a farm shop that sells fresh, home-grown fruit and veg, as well as speciality local foods. They also have an onsite coffee shop, picnic area, fishing lakes (£5 for the day) and most exciting of all – a maize maze to keep youngsters entertained for hours.

Nanny State Alert The swimming-pool area is protected by gates to keep unaccompanied children away. Unlike the ice-cream freezer in the shop.

Getting There From the A47 between Norwich and Great Yarmouth, take the A1064 at Acle (Caister-on-Sea road). Take the first left at Clippesby onto the B1152 and follow the signs to 'Clippesby Hall'.

Public Transport Catch a train to Acle and the site owners will be able to pick you up from the station if you book in advance.

Open April–Oct.

The Damage Prices for car, tent and 2 kids range from £15 in low season to £30 in high season. Dogs on leads are permitted (£3.50).

Clippesby Hall, Hall Lane, Clippesby, Norfolk NR29 3BL

| t 01493 367800 | w www.clippesby.com | 26 on the map |

manor farm

Think back to when you were a child. Remember the excitement of arriving on holiday and being able to glimpse the distant sea for the first time? All the pitches at Manor Farm have views of the sea. You can't get much more holiday than that.

Your arrival at Manor Farm is just the thing for creating the right atmosphere. To get to the site you have to drive through a farm gate that runs between cobbled and flint barns, and then up a track with hedges brushing your car on both sides. The camping fields are at the top of the hill, with the seaside town of Cromer a mere 10 minutes' walk away. And in the distance, like an ironed-out pancake, you'll see the sea.

It's a good view, and feels like a suitably remote spot to pitch your tent, even though you can walk to Cromer. The fact that you reach it via the farm track and there are no roads near by mean you can let the kids run wild without worrying too much about traffic thundering past. And while it's a pretty site, it's far from being twee, so avoiding the blazer-clad crowds of 'Chelsea-on-Sea' at Brancaster.

Manor Farm is a family-owned working farm, so there are lambs and calves to see if you happen to be visiting at Easter, and ponies to pet all year round. The place feels wild, and yet you have all the advantages of a small seaside town on your doorstep. We can think of few nicer places to spend your hols.

manor farm

The Upside Rolling fields with the sea on the horizon, and both a seaside town and the seaside itself within walking distance.

The Downside The rolling fields mean that a few of the pitches are slightly sloped.

The Facilities There are 250 standard and serviced pitches, spread across 18 acres. Marlpit and Moll's Meadow are the fields that also take caravans, and Gurney's Plantation is just for caravans and tourers. The site feels sprawling, but the facilities are never too far away, with 2 shower blocks in each field. One block has a family shower and one has a family shower room. There are also 2 laundry rooms with coin-operated washing machines and dryers. Freezers are provided.

Onsite Fun Children love the space at Manor Farm, and the gently undulating fields are great for running around in. There's also a small play area and a field for football and ball games. Children are welcome to look at the farm animals.

Offsite Fun The beaches at Cromer and Sheringham are the main local attractions, and you can walk through the site into the village, with its pretty green, swings and slides, to the beach at East Runton. The beach is pretty quiet, with good rock pools and nice views to Cromer pier. It's a sweet, old-fashioned village, with a butcher, tea room, fish-and-chip shop, even an excellent Army Surplus store and a hairdresser, so all essentials covered if you are suddenly struck with a desire to get a perm. You can catch the North Norfolk Railway, a steam train in Sheringham going to Weybourne and Holt.

If it Rains The Muckleburgh Collection (01263 588210; www.muckleburgh.co.uk) at Weybourne, with a fearsome array of tanks and fighting planes, is just up the road. There's a shirehorse centre in East Runton (01263 514902; www.eastruntonbandb. co.uk), Splash Leisure Centre in Sheringham (01263 825675) and a play barn just near Aylsham (01263 734108; www.aylshamfunbarns.co.uk). Cromer has a Movieplex (01263 510151; www.merlincinemas. co.uk) with 4 screens and a Funstop indoor play centre (01263 823150; www.norfolkbouncycastles. co.uk). At Blickling Hall (01263 738030; www. nationaltrust.org.uk), the headless ghost of Anne Boleyn is supposed to haunt the corridors.

Food & Drink Cromer is packed with fish-and-chip shops and old-fashioned cafés. The Victorian Tea Room (01263 517154) on Meadow Road is one of the best. Mary Jane's is the prime place for fish and chips, but closest to the site is Station House in Cromer. The Pepperpot Restaurant (01263 837578) in West Runton is fantastic, but more expensive. For local meat try Icarus Hines the butcher (01263 514541), in Cromer, or Arthur's butchers in West Runton; and there's also a farm shop at Groveland Farm in Roughton (01263 833777).

Nanny State Alert Although you are well away from the main road, this is a working farm with farm traffic.

Getting There Take the A149 into the village from Cley and turn left by the brown-and-white site sign saying 'Manor Farm'. Follow the road just into the village and the site is on the right-hand side.

Public Transport Catch a train to Cromer. The site is only a 10-minute walk away, though reception is another half mile away.

Open Easter–end Oct.

The Damage Standard pitch for family of 4, £14 low season, £17 high season. Serviced pitch (with hook-up) for family of 4 is £17.50 low season, £19.50 high season.

Manor Farm Caravan and Camping Site, East Runton, Cromer, Norfolk NR27 9PR

t 01263 512858   w www.manorfarmcaravansite.co.uk   27 on the map

kelling heath

Dream of a patchwork quilt of heathland, woodland
and wild-flower meadows criss-crossed by cycle tracks and
nature walks. And the sea is just at the bottom of the hill, too.
You could spend a week here without ever wanting to leave
the site – except, perhaps, to fetch ice creams.

Sitting on 250 acres of the north Norfolk Coast, the site at Kelling Heath is in a designated area of outstanding natural beauty, so don't be put off by the rather hulking red-brick area around reception. The rest of the site is lovely and is arranged sympathetically for the happiest-possible camping.

This area of the coast has a dark-sky policy, so at night the site is wonderfully inky because of the lack of glaring lights found in municipal sites. There are lots of local beaches, but the onsite fun is particularly good at Kelling, where it has an educational angle, but it's not too much like school, so your kids won't feel cheated out of having a holiday. The Acorn Club, for budding naturalists, sounds like good fun – and it is. The cycling and walking is great, and as well as playing *boules*, table tennis, swimming in the two pools and using the tennis courts, the children can go off to take part in a bug-watch and, er, beetle-drive. (Not that we know what a beetle-drive is.)

There's also an evening kids' club offering loads of activities including pond-dipping, wildlife walks, nightjar- and bat-watching and astronomy. So, studying, watching and learning are what it's all about at Kelling Heath. And eating ice creams.

kelling heath

The Upside Lovely big camping fields with sea views and lots of onsite fun.

The Downside The large red-brick central area is a bit *Brookside*.

The Facilities 300 pitches, with 3 different styles, depending on whether you want hook-ups and waste, water and TV connection. The pitches are spread over several fields, broken up with pine trees and mature woodland, so it never feels crowded. There are also lodges, but separate from the camping areas. There is a token-operated launderette, and each field has its own amenity building, with all facilities. During early autumn and spring the blocks are also heated.

Onsite Fun Onsite activities have been well thought out. As well as self-guided trails through the park, there's a marked nature trail, history trail, cycle trail and easy-access trail. There are also 2 play areas and table-tennis tables, plus bikes for hire. There's an outdoor pool and an indoor pool (entry via day pass: adult £10, child £5) and you can arrange swimming lessons. There's a gym, sauna, jacuzzi and steam room, too. The Acorn Club is a nature club for 4–12-year-olds (under-8s must be accompanied), with activities, outdoor games plus craft activities. There's also an evening kids' club.

Offsite Fun If you do leave the site, you'll find yourself on a well-equipped coastline. The North Norfolk Railway stops at the heath (request stop, so be sure to wave to the driver). West along the coast is the vast expanse of Holkham beach. Towards Kelling you will hit the marshy expanses of Morston (perfect for crabbing), and you can get sailing lessons on the quay or take a trip to see the seals (01263 740505; www.beansboattrips.co.uk). At Cley visit the windmill (01263 740209; www.cleymill. co.uk), with some cracking views of Blakeney Point (08450 946112; www.blakeneyonline.co.uk) and inland to the south are the Broads.

If it Rains Great Yarmouth (www.great-yarmouth. co.uk) has fairground rides, a circus and a cinema. Norfolk is heaving with grand piles, and Felbrigg Hall (01263 837444) is nice to explore, as is Blickling Hall (01263 738030).

Food & Drink The Dun Cow pub in Salthouse (01263 740467; www.theduncow-salthouse.co.uk) is good and the portions are huge. Cookie's Crab Shop (01263 740352), also in Salthouse, offers prawn sandwiches, lobster salad, teas and coffee. Stock up on picnic requirements at Picnic Fayre at Cley, with excellent, though expensive, food. The Smokehouse, in the village, is also a great place for kippers, potted shrimps and dressed crab, as well as fresh fish. Hills Home Stores in Blakeney is good for provisions. Don't miss out on Wiveton Hall Café (01263 740515; www.wivetonhall.co.uk) on the main road between Cley and Blakeney. Go to Salthouse beach for Julian Searjeant's fresh coffee and hot chocolate from the back of a cute French 2CV.

Nanny State Alert Watch the open water at the fishing ponds and steep descents on Cromer Ridge.

Getting There From Holt, turn left into Sandy Lane just before the village of Bodham. You will see a sign 'The Forge Kelling Heath' pointing left before the junction. Continue down Sandy Lane and the entrance to the site is on the left. Carry on down the long drive until you reach the village square, and park on your left.

Public Transport Very limited. Take the train to Sheringham then hop into a taxi. The site is happy to provide details of local taxi firms if you phone ahead.

Open Mid-Feb–mid-Dec.

The Damage £16–25 per pitch.

Kelling Heath Holiday Park, Weybourne, Holt, Norfolk NR25 7HW

t 01263 588181   w www.kellingheath.co.uk   28 on the map

high sand creek

Lick your lips as you crawl out of your tent and you will almost be able to taste the sea, just beyond the purple haze of lavender-covered marshes. Just think *Swallows and Amazons*, and you'll get the right idea – they would have loved the rich opportunities for crabbing here.

Holidays straight out of *Swallows and Amazons* spring to mind at High Sand Creek campsite in Stiffkey on the north Norfolk coast. With miles of marshes just outside your tent, the potential for a real-live adventure is huge. The site itself is very pared-down, but that doesn't mean that your opportunities for a top family holiday are limited. Plus the flat, slightly melancholic, beauty of the marshes, shimmering with dusky purple marsh heather, is magnetic.

The site has been in the same family for 40 years, and is much loved by families, who return year after year with multiple generations tacked on to augment their numbers. This stretch of the Norfolk coast is heaving with things for kids and grannies to do together. Families love the fact that there are so many opportunities for swimming and picnicking, and there's also crabbing, sailing, fishing and seal-watching to keep everyone fully occupied.

To top it off, at the end of the day, with salt in your hair, you can go to sleep safe in the knowledge that there's nothing at all between you and the North Sea.

high sand creek

The Upside Romantic and picturesque marshes, and beyond that the sea; just outside your tent.

The Downside It's not the biggest site, so at busy times there isn't a huge amount of space.

The Facilities 80 marked pitches spread over about 5 acres. No hook-ups, as the aim is to keep the site as old-fashioned as possible. There's a laundry for sink-washing clothes (but no washing machines), and 12 clean showers and 12 toilets divided into male and female blocks. Gas is available for sale, and there's a freeze-pack service.

Onsite Fun Part of the site is given over to ball games, and toys, tennis racquets, footballs and such like are available in reception. You can also borrow crabbing nets and buy bags of bait. The thick hedge that separates the site from the marshes is a favourite spot for children to explore.

Offsite Fun The coastal marsh is a haven for migrating birds, so expect to see a few twitchers twitching on the horizon. The Norfolk Coastal Path passes through Stiffkey, so the site's popular with walkers. A bridge across a creek, just beyond the site, is a prime spot for crabbing. The creeks onto the marsh are muddy, so this is great for mudlarking. Further afield is Bressingham Steam and Gardens (01379 686900; www.bressingham.co.uk) near Diss, with a great selection of vintage engines and 3 narrow-gauge railway rides around the gardens there. Go Ape! High Wire Forest Adventure (08456 439162; www.goape.co.uk) is brilliant for the over-10s, with swings, zip wires and rope bridges to test your mettle. Hunstanton, on the West coast, is a classic Victorian resort with stripy cliffs and a good beach for rock pools and exploring.

If it Rains Gressenhall Farm and Workhouse (01362 860563; www.museums.norfolk.gov.uk) has a traditional farmhouse, cottages and village shop, and an adventure playground and cart rides around the farm. There's a leisure centre at Hunstanton, as well as a Sea Life Sanctuary, with a good aquarium and otter and penguin sanctuaries. There's a play centre in Wells, with a ball pool, and cinemas in Cromer and Fakenham. The Thursford Collection (01328 878477) near Fakenham is a wonderful selection of steam engines and Victorian fair rides, and Houghton Hall (01485 528569; www.houghtonhall.com) is an impressively grand place to shelter from the rain.

Food & Drink The village shop stocks basic groceries. The Red Lion Pub is within walking distance and does good food; there's also a playground near by (01328 830552; www.stiffkey.com). There's often a fish stand at Morston for local cockles, and there are excellent dressed crabs for sale in Blakeney. Wiveton Hall Café, just beyond Blakeney, does exceptionally good food, almost all grown locally; the artichoke bruschetta and raspberry pannacotta are particularly good.

Nanny State Alert There are muddy creeks across the marshes that could be dangerous for smaller children. Also beware the marsh tides – check the tide table displayed in the warden's kiosk.

Getting There Take the A149 into Stiffkey village. Go through the village, with the sea on your right. The site is just after the Red Lion pub on the right.

Public Transport Catch a train to Sheringham or Kings Lynn, then a Coasthopper bus (no 35) to Stiffkey. Hop off opposite the post office, and walk down Bridge Street.

Open March/April–Oct.

The Damage Family of 4 costs £12–16, depending on the season.

High Sand Creek Campsite, Vale Farm, The Greenway, Stiffkey, Norfolk NR23 1QP

t 01328 830235

29 on the map

residential camps

Your kids will love a bit of independence in the summer hols – learning a few new skills and having fun together.

Going off to camp used to conjure up images of an all-American ideal of vacations, with high-kicking girls waving pom-poms like cheerleaders, and the slightly confusing idea that John Travolta or Patrick Swayze might be standing in the wings somewhere, teaching dancing to the older teenagers.

But that was probably a long, long time ago, like the seventies or something, and since then residential camps for children and teenagers have been growing in popularity in Britain, too. Longer working hours mean that fewer of us actually get to spend the whole summer with our children, and the question of how you're going to entertain them for six weeks can be an emotional and logistical nightmare for working parents.

Some of the very big, chain camps do have a depressingly corporate and soulless feel to them, but what follows is a selection of the *crème-de-la-crème* of residential camps for children. So even if you have to keep your nose to the grindstone, you can be safe in the knowledge that your children are, at least, having a fantastic time messing about in boats or learning how to survive in the wilderness, without you.

The Borrowdale Summer Camp

A stellar camp for robust children and young teenagers who are up for a challenge. Children learn proper skills like foraging, fly-fishing, first aid and mountaineering, and at the end of the week they all go off for a two-day survival expedition with Jockey. Jockey's wife Kate cooks, and there's hot chocolate and marshmallows round the campfire every evening. They've been known to set up a cinema tent and a yurt for indoor fun, too. These guys are the real McCoy.

Escape Adventures Ltd, Barclays Bank Chambers, Market Square, Keswick, Cumbria A12 5BJ; 07771 783336; www.keswickoutdoors.com; £375 per week.

The House!

If you think you've got no chance of sending your world-weary teenagers to residential camp, then The House! might be all the persuading they need. Run by Camp Beaumont, this is a camp with edge. The youngish staff ('reps') help with teen activities including urban art, quad-biking, fencing and jewellery-making, ensuring teenagers are kept interested and don't try to sneak off to carry out their own illicit activities. There's plenty of time for socialising, too, with parties on the beach and masked balls, so everyone's guaranteed to make lots of new friends, too.

Overstrand Hall, 48 Cromer Road, Overstrand, Norfolk NR27 0JJ; 01603 660333; www.campbeaumont.co.uk; £439–489 per week.

Over the Wall

This special camp, for children affected by serious illness or disability, allows them to take part in activities they might participate in at a conventional camp, such as archery, climbing, riding, fishing or canoeing. Offering respite for parents, it also gives sick children a chance to have fun in an environment with other kids facing the same sort of challenges. Run by volunteers and open to 8–17-year-olds, onsite medics make sure that the children are well cared for. This organisation is truly inspirational; they even run camps for the siblings of sick children, to give them a break.

Charwell House, Wisom Road, Alton, Hants GU34 2PP; 01420 82086; www.otw.org.uk; free, including travel.

Wickedly Wonderful

If you dream of your children spending the summer taking part in old-fashioned fun such as sailing, riding, crabbing, scavenger-hunts, picnics and making bonfires, then Wickedly Wonderful is the sort of living Boden catalogue that you're dreaming of. The children, aged 6–13, camp in their own tents in the grounds of a big house near Chichester. They put up and prepare the tents themselves, and then share them with a friend. There's no end of fun, with talent contests, jelly-fights and picnics galore, all run by some lovely girls who are happy to give the kids a bit of a cuddle if they get a little homesick.

Nr Chichester, West Sussex; 07941 231168;
www.wickedlywonderful.com; £495 for 5 days/4 nights.

Mill on the Brue

A family-run, not-for-profit educational organisation, this camp has been going strong for a quarter of a century. Run for 8–15-year-olds, there's a subtle emphasis on equipping the youngsters with some pretty essential life-skills, such as problem-solving and team work. The food is especially good and, where possible, is locally and organically produced. Food that has not come from the kitchen garden has the number of food miles travelled on view, so children are really encouraged to think about their environment.

Trendle Farm, Somerset BA10 0BA; 01749 812307;
www.millonthebrue.co.uk; £499 per week.

The Venture Centre

One of the longest-established camps in the country, this camp has been in the Reed family for 25 years and they certainly know their stuff when it comes to keeping kids happy. Originally entirely based around water activities – sailing, kayaking, rafting, canoeing, power-boating – they have more recently branched out to include activities such as mountain-biking, gorge-walking, archery and general survival, with emphasis still firmly on outdoor activities. Each camp is for about 30 children, sleeping in small dormitories, and runs for five days. There are numerous repeat bookings, with some children returning five or six years in a row.

Lewaigue Farm, Maughold, Isle of Man IM7 1AW; 01624 814240; www.adventure-centre.co.uk; £220 for 5 days.

bosworth

Grab your buckets and spades, kids –
we're off to Warwickshire! Not located in a county
immediately associated with a stunning coastline,
Bosworth Water Trust, with its small sandy
beach by the lake, is quite a find.

If you and your brood fancy an action-packed trip, head for Bosworth Water Trust campsite, on a 50-acre country park with 20 acres of water sports. Probably pretty uniquely for a campsite – particularly in this neck of the woods – it has kayaking, windsurfing, sailing and canoeing. And you don't need to splash out on any fancy kit. The campsite will hire out everything you need in the way of tackle and togs, and runs sailing, windsurfing and power-boating courses.

If you are feeling less adventurous (or energetic), you will find rowing boats and pedalos, and you can fish from dawn to dusk.

A small sandy 'beach' next to the lake's roped-off swimming zone should keep younger bods happy building sandcastles, and in keeping with the seaside theme (if not strictly *Cool Camping*-style) the park has a pirate-ship playground, crazy golf, dodgems and bungee jumping. After all this, if you're still in the market for more, the campsite has a volleyball net.

When you're finally ready for a sit-down, the café has tables overlooking the lake, and as the campsite only takes families and couples the absence of groups means you get a well-earned good night's sleep come shut-eye time.

bosworth

The Upside It might be in the landlocked Midlands, but it has a beach.

The Downside The dodgems are a bit incongruous and the caravan-to-tent ratio is about 50:50. The showers can't always cope with all those wet people, but there are plans to extend the block.

The Facilities The site has marked hook-up pitches, and unmarked pitches for tents without hook-ups over 2 large, flat fields, with plenty of space around pitches. There are 2 toilet/shower blocks, one of which is on the campsite, and the other near the shop (also for day-trippers using the lake). The campsite block has 3 showers and 3 toilets each for men and women. A further toilet and shower block next to the shop also has a disabled toilet with shower and basin. The shop is open from 8.30am to 7pm or 10pm (depending on season) and sells toys, games, ice creams, crisps and bits and pieces you might have forgotten – like batteries and toothbrushes.

Onsite Fun At the pay-and-play Saturday Kids' Club (10am–12.30pm) (book a week in advance on 01455 291876) kids aged 8 and over get the chance to try sailing, kayaking and windsurfing. There is a small swimming area roped off, a sandy area for sandcastle-building and fishing (£2 for a day ticket). The country park has pirate-ship-theme play equipment, dodgems (operating at busy periods), bungee jumping and crazy golf.

Offsite Fun Twycross Zoo (01827 880250; www.twycrosszoo.com) is about 20 minutes down the road, or visit Bosworth Battlefield Heritage Centre and Country Park (01455 290429; www.bosworthbattlefield.com) for the story of the 1485 battle of Bosworth. The Battlefield Line Railway (01827 880754; www.battlefield-line-railway.co.uk) runs from Shackerstone station (15 minutes away).

If it Rains Snibston Discovery Park (combining science, transport and mining) (01530 278444) is in Coalville (about half an hour away) and Conkers in the National Forest (01283 216633; www.visitconkers.com) is almost an hour away on the B586 (Rawdon Road) in Moira, near Ashby-de-la-Zouche. Both have indoor and outdoor areas with hands-on activities.

Food & Drink Onsite, Bruschetta's Café Bar (01455 292685) serves up big breakfasts, jacket potatoes, sandwiches and daily specials. Market Bosworth is within walking distance and has a fish-and-chip shop, cafés (including Café Torte selling local ice cream, ciabattas and cakes) and the Black Horse Inn (01455 290278; www.theblackhorserestaurant.co.uk) with home-made gastro-style food.

Nanny State Alert You need to supervise children swimming, as lifeguards may be attending other parts of the lake.

Getting There Half a mile west of Market Bosworth, on the B585, the country park entrance is signed from the road.

Public Transport A bus stops 200 metres from the site entrance, and buses run from Hinckley and Leicester to Market Bosworth.

Open All year.

The Damage £12 per night in the low season (Oct–May) rising to £14 (June–Sept and Bank Holiday weekends) for a tent. Families and couples over 23 only. You also need change on arrival – £3 (or £4 Sundays and Bank Holidays) – to operate the barrier when you first arrive at the country park. A barrier card is issued once you've checked in, for a £10 refundable deposit.

Bosworth Water Trust, Far Coton Lane, Wellsborough Rd, Nr Nuneaton, Warwickshire CV13 6PD

t 01455 291876   w www.bosworthwatertrust.co.uk   30 on the map

talton lodge

Do you and your kids feel like having a little TLC?
Here's a place to cocoon your family in an idyllic world –
just for a weekend. And it's a kids' utopia: a mouth-
watering combination of tents and food – all enclosed in a
cosy Victorian walled garden.

Talton Lodge has the ultimate secret garden that you can just disappear into. When the latched wooden gate is opened you'll be sure to gasp with excitement at the sight in front of you (rather like the beginning of a theme park ad, but without the schmaltz).

The campsite is in a Victorian red-brick walled garden, with all the bits and pieces you'd expect: veggie patches, raspberry bushes, chicken coops, an orchard – all topped off with a babbling brook. You'll find tipis, a yurt and a shower pavilion, surrounded by all sorts of self-sufficiency, from soft fruit to hand-reared heavenly hog. A truly amazing find.

The Norwegian tipi on the lawn is huge (vast enough to hold a wedding for 65). And just across the gravel path you'll find a traditionally decorated Mongolian yurt. Behind the cast-iron gates, just beyond the wall, you'll be able to glimpse the top of a traditional North American tipi.

The garden is a kids' paradise – being able to run in and out of trees and tipis. And there's a further 20 acres surrounding this. Throw in Olivia's home produce – and you'd be mad not to take advantage of her cooking at least once during your stay. You won't be able to help feeling completely relaxed at Talton. A divine experience.

talton lodge

The Upside Luxurious yurt and tipi accommodation. Beautiful countryside and a river. Magical location.

The Downside Technically there are only 2 sleeping 'tents', but there are already plans for a third canvas structure in the walled garden, plus more tipis in the woods. They are also converting a barn, which will take 5 people.

The Facilities One tipi, tucked away by the stream, sleeps a couple plus 2 kids (snugly). A beautiful hand-painted traditional Mongolian yurt sleeps 7, plus baby (travel cot provided). It has a double bed, singles and a sofa bed. There are cosy wood-burners and a traditional chamber-pot in each tent for emergencies. The huge Norwegian tipi functions as a living space, with fridge, gas cooker, microwave and comfy chairs around a fire pit (an old washing-machine drum). It has crockery and cutlery, plus tea, coffee and cooking oil. The 'Pavilion' houses a huge wet-room with loo, one for girls, one for boys, with washing-up sink. There's even a daybed to lounge on if you have to wait.

Onsite Fun Running around the orchard, feeding the pigs, playing Pooh Sticks or tennis, canoeing, swimming and fishing in the river. After dark enjoy spotting foxes, mink and even, perhaps, the elusive Newbold panther!

Offsite Fun Cycling off to explore the beautiful Warwickshire countryside. Given notice Olivia will meet you with a beyond-scrumptious food hamper. Younger children will love the maize maze at Hidcote (07974 487861; www.hidcotemaze.co.uk).

If it Rains Stoke up the fire pit in the Norwegian tipi and enjoy the sound of raindrops on canvas, while reading the handbook on 'How to construct a traditional Mongolian yurt'. There's 65 people's worth of space and a huge table for kids to do drawing and leaf-sticking. There's a games room with table football. If you feel the need to get into a car, Warwick Castle (0870 4422000; www.warwick-castle.co.uk) has ramparts, battles, gift shop – that sort of thing.

Food & Drink Olivia provides her own free-range eggs (so free you might find that a chicken has actually laid one in your egg-cup), preserves, bread, sausages and ham, plus veg and fruit in season. Best option is to buy one of Olivia's breakfast boxes, cook melt-in-the-mouth sausages for the kids' tea, get them tucked up, then get Olivia to serve you a 3-course dinner. There's also a fully stocked farm shop just up the lane. There are 2 family-friendly pubs in the village, an adult 5-minute walk away: the White Hart (01789 450205) and the Bird in Hand (01789 450253).

Nanny State Alert If soft fruit is in season, there's a chance your kids (and not just the kids) could seriously over-gorge themselves. Watch out for cherry-stained chops and sticky raspberry-mitts.

Getting There At Newbold-on-Stour (on the A3400), follow the sign opposite the Post Office for Adrington and Crimscote. Drive for a few minutes along a country lane and Talton Lodge is on the left.

Public Transport The nearest train station is Moreton-in-Marsh, which is a 10-minute taxi ride from the site. You can also get the train to Stratford-on-Avon, then do the 20-minute journey by bus, which leaves hourly and takes you to the end of the road, ¼ mile from the site.

Open April–Oct.

The Damage £80 a night for up to 4 people and £100 a night for up to 6 in the tipi/yurt, with discount for more than 2 nights. Car-less people get 2 days' free bike hire. Snooker, tennis and bike hire £10.

Talton Lodge, Newbold-on-Stour, Warwickshire CV37 8UB

| t 07962 273417 | w www.taltonlodge.co.uk | 31 on the map |

tresseck

There's plenty of watery fun to please all ages at this no-frills site in a lush green meadow on the banks of the River Wye. Imagine bangers 'n' beans sizzling while you crack open a well-earned beer at the end of an action-packed day in a canoe on the river.

Once discovered, always a fan, it seems, since this site has plenty of campers who come back again and again. They love the 'no delusions of grandeur' vibe. It's a field by some water. But what water.

Whether it's messing about in boats, splashing, paddling or just admiring this great expanse of river, the Wye will quickly have you hooked, like one of the local salmon on a fisherman's rod. Everyone rubs along nicely here – from couples holed up in cosy two-man ridges, to groups of families in their domes, to the ever-present canoeists making the most of the landing site by the tiny beach.

Human traffic eases off during the day as campers paddle, wander or drive off to follow their respective pursuits. But by four-ish most are back in the fold again, relishing the relaxed environment. Watery tales are swapped and blistered fingers patched up. With a family-friendly pub by the gate and two more close by, what's not to like?

Whatever time you choose to climb into your sleeping bag, you can be assured that you'll fall asleep to the crackle of open fires, the swishing of water in the reeds, the cough of a sheep and laughter from the pub garden. Quite a lullabye!

tresseck

The Upside Watching the river go by (and the array of wildlife and floating or capsizing vessels on it). A horizontally laid-back atmosphere, with open fires.

The Downside Sadly there's a music ban, due to neighbours threatening to close the site, so it's vital to respect this.

The Facilities There are 4 cold taps, several portaloos, but no showers, so clean-freaks need not apply. The large rubbish skip is extremely useful, if not exactly enhancing the beauty of the, frankly, stunning surroundings. This is a tent-only site, though camper vans are welcomed into the fold, as long as they don't need electricity. Tresseck does have fishing rights, so ask for details when booking.

Onsite Fun The camp field is a ball-tastic throwing and kicking space. There's a sheltered landing spot for canoeists, but even if you're a confirmed land-lubber there's a great deal of pleasure to be had from watching people squeezing themselves in and out of their vessels (ooh – and sometimes falling in!). Otherwise pander to desires for paddling, wild swimming and fishing.

Offsite Fun This is picture-postcard territory. Wander around the lanes and footpaths. Play Pooh Sticks off the bridge around the corner. Check out the Italian church. Mess about in boats. Canoeing to Ross-on-Wye will take about 3½ hours, so you may want to arrange a pick-up with one of the ever-helpful local companies (01432 873020; www.herefordcanoehire.com and 01600 891199; www.wye-pursuits.co.uk). Get lost in the Symonds Yat maze (01600 890360; www.mazes.co.uk).

If it Rains Goodrich Castle (01600 890538; www.english-heritage.org.uk) is a stunning ruin just west of Ross, with roll-downable grassy banks and towers to climb. Puzzlewood (01594 833187; www.puzzlewood.net) in the Forest of Dean has an indoor wood puzzle maze and animals to pet. When the rain abates experience running around the 15 acres of moss-covered paths, reputed to have been Tolkien's inspiration for *Lord of the Rings*.

Food & Drink The New Harp Inn is literally on your doorstep (01432 840900; www.newharpinn.co.uk), so you can check it out before booking. The Lough Pool Inn (01989 730236; www.loughpool.co.uk) is only a 10-minute walk away in Sellack and the Cottage of Content (01432 840242; www.cottageofcontent.co.uk), which offers colouring-in equipment for small ones (and lifts for those without cars), is a 5-minute drive in the opposite direction. Nearby Ross-on-Wye offers a Morrison's supermarket, Audrey's Fish Bar (01989 563821) and Pan Pizza (01989 562288), which will deliver. Result. Ruth, who owns Tresseck, visits at 8am every morning and can sell you firewood. She'll even get you milk if you're desperate.

Nanny State Alert You are camping right by a beautiful but fast-moving river. If this worries you with small kids about, pitch in the top end of the field, where there's a fence between the site and the river.

Getting There From Ross-on-Wye take the A49 north. Take the second right, signposted 'Hoarwithy'. Follow the country lane for 4 miles and you'll find yourself by the New Harp Inn in the centre of Hoarwithy. The campsite entrance is immediately past the pub on the right.

Public Transport Nearest train station is Hereford. From there take the number 37 bus, which drops you right outside the pub. You can also get the 37 from Ross.

Open Easter–end Sept.

The Damage Adults £4, children £2.

Tresseck Campsite, Hoarwithy, Herefordshire HR2 6QJ

t 01432 840235　　w www.tresseckcampsite.co.uk　　32 on the map

woodland tipis and yurts

Do your kids dream of elves and fairies, or cowboys and indians? They will when you've tucked them up snug in a cosy Woodland tipi or yurt, and read them a story in front of the glowing embers of a wood fire, after a day running wild in the woods.

Rules and regulations don't exist at Woodland. Freedom reigns. There are no signs telling your kids not to kick a ball, walk on the grass or make too much noise, though doggy friends should be left behind. And with a visitors' book bursting with endless vows from others to come back, you'll probably find it's a cut above any camping experience you've ever had.

Arrive, dump your belongings into a wheelbarrow. Wheel. Unpack your cool bag into your fridge, fling your duvets onto the comfy beds, light a fire – and relax. Revel in the fact that your children can run free in six acres of (totally car-free) stunning woodland. No DVDs needed here. Whimsical touches add to the whole inside–outside feel – children's party bunting hangs in the trees, jam jars of wild flowers are scattered about. The roll-top bath with its Cath Kidston styling is perfect for pre-bed bathtime for babes and tots – and even more perfect for you to chill out in, with a glass or two, later.

If cooking outdoors isn't you, there's a utensil-packed kitchen and fairy lights for that oooh factor after dark. So, if frozen pizza from an electric oven is your bag – you're sorted, but chances are that by day two you'll be making fresh pizza in the wood-fired bread oven.

woodland tipis and yurts

The Upside Luxury cool camping in a magical woodland setting.

The Downside You may have to drag your family kicking and screaming when it's time to check out.

The Facilities The 3 yurts and 3 tipis each sleep 4–5 on comfortable mattresses strewn with sheepskin rugs. Bring sleeping bags/duvets and linen. Each has an in-tent gas-stove and wood-burner. Outside you'll find your own hammock, fireplace and dining space. There's a communal kitchen with electricity, fuelling fridges, energy-saving kettles and cookers. On the cooking front, though, the *pièce de résistance* has to be the massive clay oven – so huge it has its own little house, complete with armchairs. Send your offspring into the woods on a fuel-finding mission, while you sit close by with a glass of something – and watch the flames rise. The shared loos and showers are immaculate and the ultimate in cool. For the greenest option, there's one composting loo tucked away in the bushes. Woodland have thought of everything for little people, as there's a travel cot, available on request, as well as 2 retro-style highchairs in the kitchen. And if you're not keen on hand-washing, machine facilities are available.

Onsite Fun Running wild in the woods, making dens, swinging on old tyres and rope ladders. Making home-made biscuits in the clay oven. Playing in the sand-pit. Pushing your friends around in a wheelbarrow.

Offsite Fun You're only a hop, skip or a jump away from the stunning River Wye. Enjoy paddling on tiny pebbly beaches, wobbling on the swing-bridge or kayaking. Outdoor activities abound, from Pedalbikeaway Cycles (01600 772821) to Severnvale Llama and Donkey Trekking (01594 528482).

If it Rains Check out the visitors' book for loads of recommendations, including the grandeur of Eastnor Castle (01531 633160) and underground adventures at Clearwell Caves (01594 832535). For those needing a bit of sophistication (and a latté or two), swing by the Baileys café and über-chic interiors barn, 10 minutes down the road at Bridstow (www.baileyshomeandgarden.co.uk).

Food & Drink You can buy bread, milk and basic supplies onsite. Stock up on fresh, local produce and booze at the Pengethley farm shop (01989 730430) in nearby Peterstow. You're spoilt for choice with 3 nearby pubs, all offering gastro-pub-style family-friendly food and drink. The New Harp Inn (01432 840900) is less than 10 minutes' walk through the wood in Hoarwithy, the Cottage of Content (01432 840242) is 5 minutes' drive away in Carey and the Lough Pool Inn (01989 730236) is 5 minutes' drive in the opposite direction, at Sellack.

Nanny State Alert Apart from falling off a tree swing, or tripping over a guy rope, there's little for even the most anxious of parents to worry about here. A 'no cars inside the campsite' policy means kids of all ages can dash about willy-nilly.

Getting There Details on booking. Located between Hoarwithy and Little Dewchurch.

Public Transport Catch the train to Hereford; bus 37 (from Hereford or Ross-on-Wye) passes by the farm every 2 hours (Young's Coaches; 01531 821584).

Open April–Sept.

The Damage Mid-week prices (4 nights) are £200 for tipis and £230/£260 for yurts. Weekend rates (3 nights) are from £220 for tipis and £270/£310 for yurts. In high season, weekly rates are £500 for tipis and £550/£590 for yurts.

Woodland Tipis and Yurts, Woodlands Farm, Little Dewchurch, Herefordshire HR2 6QD

t 01432 840488   w www.woodlandtipis.co.uk   33 on the map

yellow wood

Sleeping in a tent – pah! That's just for wimps!
Tarpaulins are the order of the day at this site.
You get the run of a real-live bush camp, made all the more
exciting by its secret location in ancient woodland.
Just don't forget to bring your Swiss army knife.

Tucked away in Herefordshire, on the edge of the Welsh borders, nestles Yellow Wood – five acres of ancient woodland surrounded by footpaths, more trees and a stunning backdrop of mountains.

If you've ever camped in the States or Down Under, you'll already get what bush-camping is all about. And this was the intention of bushman Paul when he set up the camp three years ago. This site re-writes the camping rule book. You won't find a shop that'll freeze your cool blocks or top-up your camping gas here. Certainly not. Yellow Wood is all about appreciating and learning how to work in harmony with your surroundings and getting down and dirty with nature. Party central this ain't. There's a quiet policy from 11pm until 7am – so campers (as well as all the little furry fellas you'll no doubt be sharing the wood with, perched up in trees or tucked down burrows) can fully appreciate their natural surroundings. Families who've stayed before have made signs for some of the pitches, so if you're feeling adventurous you could opt for Wolf's Retreat – or dream up your own name.

Yellow Wood is the ultimate back-to-nature experience – and like those who've been here before you, you'll be completely hooked.

yellow wood

The Upside Cooking on open fires. Creating your own camp, then sleeping under the stars in a hammock or on a groundsheet under a tarpaulin.

The Downside No pets allowed, but you can make friends with a fox, wild rabbit or perhaps just a spider.

The Facilities There are 17 pitches nestled in the wood, but these are rotated, so you won't be camping on top of anyone else. The pitch size varies to suit groups of 6, 4 and 2 people. There's one composting loo (whistle if you hear anyone coming) and a men's bush urinal. More are planned. If your family dome tent is dull, hire a tarpaulin or even a tipi. For a refreshing start to the day, try the bush-shower dash – though if you're feeling precious, warm up the water first. Firewood is available at £5 per wheelbarrow. Don't even think about burning fallen branches – every twig is part of the delicate ecosystem. Paul runs bushcraft courses. You'll learn how to identify edible plants and light fires in all weathers without matches. These are an optional extra, but he's only a call away if you do need the benefit of his know-how.

Onsite Fun Once you've experienced the excitement of rigging up your camp in the trees, there's cooking on open fires, tree-clambering and nature-walking. Adapt, or make your own, bush furniture – draining-boards or chairs – from twigs lashed together with binder-twine. Love the sounds of a wood in full swing: leaves falling, twigs snapping, birds twittering.

Offsite Fun Handily, there's a nature reserve right behind Yellow Wood. If you want a river walk, you're only a pleasant 1½ miles away. A fab canoeing spot is a 2½-mile walk away; several local companies offer drop-offs and pick-ups. Wye Valley Canoes (01497 847213; www.wyevalleycanoes.co.uk) are particularly amenable. The Brecon Beacons National Park (www.visit-brecon-beacons.co.uk) is only 7 miles away and offers most outdoor pursuits, from hiking to caving and kayaking.

If it Rains If rain has you running for the nearest centrally heated leisure centre, Yellow Wood isn't for you. There's a tarpaulin by the car-parking spaces, so if you arrive in the rain there's a chance to get your act together before pitching. Tree cover is usually nature's umbrella – and snuggling by a fire is the best way to dry out. If you do decide to pike out, you're only 6 miles from cultural Hay-on-Wye or 18 miles from the Odeon cinema in Hereford (08712 244007).

Food & Drink There's a pub in the village about 1 mile back down the track. There's another pub 2½ miles away by the river. Both serve good food and cater for kids. If you run out of milk there's a garage a couple of miles away. Head for Hay-on-Wye for a Co-op, greengrocers, bakers and cafés.

Nanny State Alert This is the great outdoors. Sometimes poisonous wild fungi spring up, so point out such things to your kids.

Getting There Location is top secret (to avoid overloading the delicate landscape), so you will be given directions on booking (including the secret code for the bush camp's 5-bar gate).

Public Transport Location top secret – directions on booking.

Open All year.

The Damage £5 per adult, £3 per child over 3; those under 3 are free. If you arrive by public transport, bike or on foot you'll get 10 per cent discount. Booking is essential.

Yellow Wood Bush Camp, Nr Hay-on-Wye, Herefordshire

t   0845 2261292 or text 07800 767519   w   www.yellowwood.co.uk   34   on the map

pencelli castle

A highly colourful past (lots of blood), thankfully long gone, has been replaced by a harmonious and equally colourful present (lots of flowers) at Pencelli Castle. And everything's so clean and orderly. The loos might well be even cleaner than your own loo at home.

Arriving at Pencelli Castle you are greeted with a truly psychedelic display of flowers beside the play area. Not for nothing have the site owners, the Rees family, won the Wales in Bloom campsite category for the last five years.

This is a place that is just packed full of history, though the more gory bits are now consigned to the file labelled 'historical interest'. Thankfully the bloody battles that were fought here up until the 1300s are now a thing of the distant past. The castle was around until the 1550s, when it was pulled to bits and taken to be used for local building material. But there are some shadowy reminders of its former grandeur all over the site, like bits of the old walls, or the house, which was part of the chapel until 1583.

The Reeses run the site like clockwork, and their attention to the finer details is what makes it work so well: there's a much-appreciated bike- and boot-wash, for example, and Gerwyn and his son work hard to keep the camping fields well drained to reduce the amount of tarmac onsite.

Paying quiet consideration to a camper's every need is what this dedicated family does so very well, and the reason why staying here is so very nice.

pencelli castle

The Upside Everything about this site says child-friendly, all the way from the spanking-clean loos to the generous play area to the well-clipped camping fields.

The Downside The loos are a bit of a walk if you are staying in the nicest camping field – the Meadows.

The Facilities With 80 pitches over 3 fields space rarely feels cramped, and the facilities are spick and span, with 10 award-winning showers and 2 family wash-rooms, all heated. There's a small laundry with iron, fridge-freezer and spotless washing-up facilities. There's a useful information room and you can order newspapers daily. A small shop stocks basic provisions, and there's also a place to store bikes and boots, so after a long walk you don't have to cuddle up to your muddy footwear at night.

Onsite Fun The site is very welcoming for children, and there's a good play area with a grass pitch. Children can follow the nature trail around the site, which includes the red deer enclosure and vintage farm machinery. The Brecon Beacons are only a stone's throw away and hardy campers often pitch tents here in the bleak midwinter to witness the first snow. The canal running along the side of the site means you can launch a canoe directly from the camping field.

Offsite Fun The Brecon to Monmouthshire Canal (01873 830328) runs right along the edge of the site, and you can take a boat trip on it. You can also hire day boats for 4–8 people. There is pony-trekking at Cantref (01874 665223; www.cantref.com), as well as a play farm, with pig-racing and sheep-shearing to watch. Pen y Fan, the highest point in the Brecon Beacons isn't far and is a great excursion for older kids. The Taff Trail (01639 893661; www.tafftrail.org.uk) criss-crosses this area, a network of cycle paths running along the canal and through the villages.

If it Rains There's indoor climbing at Llangorse activity centre (01874 658272; www.llangorselake.co.uk), and for a canal trip you can catch Dragonfly Cruises (07831 685222; www.dragonfly-cruises.co.uk). Saint Fagan's Welsh Folk Museum (02920 569441; www.museumwales.co.uk) is a 16th-century manor house surrounded by 40 buildings re-erected from different parts of Wales, and makes an excellent day trip.

Food & Drink 100 metres up the road is the Royal Oak pub, but the best food is found in the White Swan (01874 665276; www.the-white-swan.com) in Llanfrynach. There's a farm shop at Middle Wood, which is good for local meat. An onsite shop sells basic provisions, and if you order before 4.30pm you can have a delivery of milk and bread for the following morning. A mile away you can buy lethal local cider from Aber Valley, but if you're up early with the kids then it might be better to stick to their equally excellent, though less potent, apple juice.

Nanny State Alert Watch out for the canal that runs the length of the site.

Getting There From Abergavenny take the A40 towards Brecon. Six miles from Brecon turn left to Talybont on Usk. In the village turn right and the site is the first place you come to on the right.

Public Transport Catch a train to Abergavenny, then hop onto the Sixty-Sixty bus no X43 towards Brecon/Cardiff. The bus stops very near to the site and you can find timetables at reception for your journey home.

Open All year, except 3rd–28th Dec.

The Damage Starting from £7.50 per adult, £4 per child.

Pencelli Castle Caravan and Camping Park, Pencelli, Brecon, Powys LD3 7LX

t 01874 665451　　w www.pencelli-castle.co.uk　　35 on the map

dan-yr-ogof

Do you secretly harbour fantasies of waking up
next to a Tyrannosaurus rex? No, we didn't think so.
However, your children almost certainly do. Even if you don't
like dinosaurs (not now you're a grown-up) we know you'll
love this site right next to the Brecon Beacons.

If you had been born 200 million years ago, then you might have regularly woken up to the sound of a T. rex roaring for his brekkies. Of course, *Homo sapiens* was not actually around then, but that's beside the point. And if your children are still young and impressionable, you might be able to convince them that if they're very, very lucky, and exceptionally well behaved, they might even see a real dinosaur. A perfect solution for a nice peaceful holiday.

Dan-yr-Ogof is, to say the least, an esoteric campsite, because it's tacked onto the edge of a Dinosaur Park, complete with over 100 replicas of life-size prehistoric animals, as well as the splendidly named Showcaves, which are part of the limestone mountains. There's also a replica Iron Age Farm (well, you didn't think that it would be real did you?), a shire-horse centre and a Victorian farm, as well as fields full of dinky donkeys and some truculent llamas. You even have to walk through the legs of a Diplodocus to enter the caves.

Children love the animals and the space; grown-ups love the Brecon Beacons, and the fact that their children are having a great time. A happy holiday, therefore, can be had by all. Dan-yr-Ogof: it even sounds like the name of a yet-undiscovered dinosaur.

dan-yr-ogof

The Upside The site is sympathetically designed; families are all together in one area, with lots of room for children, and the facilities are very clean.

The Downside You'll have to walk through the legs of a diplodocus to get to the caves.

The Facilities The site is on the far side of the Showcaves and dinosaur park, so you're not actually up close and personal with a T. rex. There are 30 level pitches with one area designated for families; 10 have hook-ups. Six showers are divided equally between men and women, and there are industrial-sized washing machines (£2) and dryers (£2).

Onsite Fun The caves were discovered in 1912 by 2 local farmers who drew arrows in the sand and lit their route with candles; the caves are still a very exciting attraction, with the far-reaching main cave, a further Bone Cave (where 42 skeletons of 3,000-year-old Bronze-Age people were found) and the Cathedral Cave (impressively huge with fantastic acoustics). Set a little way from the camping site, the caves and dinosaurs are fun for half a day, but there are also fields full of animals (alpaca, lambs, shire-horses, ducks, donkey, geese and chickens).

Offsite Fun You are right next door to some of the most awesome scenery in the country, so this is a fabulous place for walking, cycling and pony-trekking; the National Park Mountain Centre (01874 623366) can advise on routes and safety. You can hire ponies for trekking at Tregoyd Mountain Riders (01497 847351; www.tregoydriding.co.uk). Craig-y-Nos Country Park (01639 730395) is a big 19th-century mock castle with 40 acres of beautiful gardens with lakes. The moated Raglan Castle (www.castlewales.com/raglan) is a nice place to picnic. Rhondda Heritage Park (01443 682036; www.rhonddaheritagepark.com) is part of a former colliery and provides interesting historical insight. If you feel inspired by mining history, there's also the Big Pit Mine near Blaenavon (01495 790311; www.museumwales.ac.uk).

If it Rains Most camping trips are characterised by at least one morning of wet weather, so you could save the caves for then. Otherwise a day out in Cardiff will take you to the Doctor Who Up Close Exhibition (02920 489257; www.doctorwhoexhibition.com). Swansea (www.swansea.gov.uk) is 18 miles away on the lovely Gower Coast and its maritime museum (01792 650351) is worth a look.

Food & Drink The nearest village shop is 3 miles away and there are several pick-your-owns at Sunny Bridge, about 7 miles away. The best local pub is the Gwyn Arms (01639 730310), but the Ancient Britton (01639 730273) and Abercrave Inn (01639 731002) are not bad either. There's a Spar shop 2 miles up the road for basics, and you can get breakfast, lunch and tea in the onsite café.

Nanny State Alert This is Wales's premier tourist attraction, and the car park is at the bottom of the site, so in busy times there are lots of cars around.

Getting There From junction 43 on the M4 take the A465 to Glyn Neath, then the A4109, on to the A4221 to Abercrave. Pick up the A4607 to Dan-yr-Ogof. The signs will guide you in.

Public Transport Happily the no 63 bus between Brecon and Swansea stops outside the main gate.

Open Easter–Oct.

The Damage £5 per adult per night and £3 per child per night.

Dan-yr-Ogof, The National Showcaves Centre for Wales, Abercrave, Glyntawe, Swansea SA9 1GJ

t 01639 730284   w www.showcaves.co.uk   36 on the map

erwlon

If you're a bit of a camping novice, then Erwlon will
help you get your tent legs. In fact, this site might turn you into
such a happy camper that you'll be striking out on a wild walk
into the mountains before you can say 'tent peg'.

There is an element of camping that is all about surprises. The surprise, for example, of finding yourself eating crisps for breakfast. Or realising you haven't had a bath for a week. Or waking up to a priceless view of a Welsh valley. And because camping can sometimes be a bit unpredictable (the moody weather, for instance) it can be rather soothing to arrive at a campsite that does exactly what it says on the tin. And that's precisely what Erwlon does.

There are no frills and no surprises to be had here, but it's a friendly, well-maintained and attractive little site in the bosom of Wales's loveliest countryside. The Rees family have been running the site since the 1950s and brothers Peter and Huw are now the third generation in a row to be involved. They have the devoted help of their dad, who still mows the lawns and tends the banks of colourful flowers you can see around the site.

Open year-round, it's a popular site with walkers who want to explore this gorgeous pocket of land on the edge of the Brecon Beacons. Clean facilities, lovely location and a friendly welcome: like we said, it does exactly what it says on the tin.

erwlon

The Upside Spanking-clean facilities, including award-winning loos and heated amenities. All set in a quiet little site snuggled up to the Brecon Beacons. More castles than you can shake a stick at.

The Downside Space can get a little tight during busy times, as the first half of the field is designated for caravans and tourers.

The Facilities You could eat your lunch off the floor of any of the 5 family rooms in the wash-block. You don't have to, of course, but these washing facilities certainly aren't the sort that you have to brace yourself to face in the mornings. The site's made up of 2 fields of 100 pitches – most have hook-ups, and there are laundry and dishwashing facilities, as well as drying-room and fridge-freezer. Wi-fi beams all over the site. Handy baby-changing facilities.

Onsite Fun At the site centre is a play area with swings, climbing frames and a fireman's pole for under-12s. Children are welcome to go (with parents) to watch the cows being milked.

Offsite Fun Ever fancied finding 3 ways to go underground in Wales? Well this is the site for you, with a tour down the Big Pit Mines (see p184), a trip to the Showcaves at Dan-yr-Ogof (see p184) and a thrilling trip to look for gold at the Dolaucothi Gold Mines (01558 825146). The trails of Cwm Rhaeadr are only a 20-minute cycle ride away. It's a fantastic place for a day out, and the area's drenched in history, including Bronze Age burial cairns and Iron Age hill forts. The cycle tracks are particularly good; you can hire bikes through the Reeses. Try out the pony-trekking at Pumpsaint and Llanwrtyd (01686 628200; www.wales-holidays.co.uk).

If it Rains Most children love dungeons, and the ones at Carreg Cennen (01558 822291; www.carregcennencastle.com) won't disappoint.

Pony-mad children will adore Cantref Adventure Farm and Riding Centre (01874 665223; www.cantref.com), where there's an indoor play zone plus pig track and sledge rides. The Heritage Centre in Llandovery (01558 824226; www.llandovery.org.uk) has displays on local myths and legends. The Heart Of Wales Railway Line passes over the awesome Cynghordy Viaduct (www.cynghordy.info) and then into a tunnel under the Sugar Loaf Mountains. Pick it up at Swansea, Llanelli or Shrewsbury.

Food & Drink You can't visit Erwlon without a trip into Llandovery to the Penygawse Victorian Tea Rooms. Beneath its tinkling chandeliers you can enjoy great lunches, excellent cream teas and the best coffee in Wales. For lipsmackingly good ice cream head to Llanfaes ice-cream parlour with 50 flavours of locally made ice cream. Thirteen miles away is the Angel pub (2-star Michelin; 01558 823394) at Salem and the Red Lion at Llangadog (01550 777357) also does great meals.

Nanny State Alert Although there's a thick hedge along the edge of the site, watch the road beside it – it's quite fast.

Getting There From the Severn Bridge, leave the M4 at Junction 24 and head North along the A449 until you join the A40 at Raglan. Head West to Llandovery. The site is just off the A40, 1 mile east of Llandovery, on the road towards Brecon on the right-hand side.

Public Transport Take a train to Swansea, then another to Llandovery. The campsite is a 10-minute walk, or there is a bus that stops at the supermarket 2 minutes from the site.

Open All year.

The Damage £13 per night for a family of 4, £16 with hook-up.

Erwlon Caravan and Camping Park, Brecon Road, Llandovery, Carmarthenshire SA20 0RD

| t | 01550 721021/720332 | w | www.erwlon.co.uk | 37 | on the map |

tir bach farm

We sincerely hope you don't get lost in the snaking lanes that twist and turn their way towards the mellow spot that is Tir Bach Farm. But we promise that once you've finally found this farmland site, you'll never want to leave. And you'll find plenty to have a laugh about there, too.

Most people have dreams. Some people dream about winning the lottery, or writing a bestselling novel. Living in Bristol, Ashley and Rose had a dream about moving to Wales to farm a smallholding and run a cute little family-friendly campsite. It takes all sorts.

They heard about Tir Bach Farm, which, appropriately, means 'small land'. And as soon as they visited this special little pocket of Wales, and met the farmer, they realised that their dream was right in front of them. All that was a few years ago. They now have not only a campsite, but also a grand collection of animals in their care: cows, breeding sows, kune kune pigs and goats, as well as geese, ducks and the odd chicken scratching around the farmyard. There's plenty of fun and exploring for children to do onsite, and there are enough local beaches and castles to keep you and your gang amused for several weeks.

One of the nicest things is that at the end of a day out you can return to the whispering stillness of Tir Bach Farm. It's a mellow spot, because Rose and Ashley are mellow people. We think that you'll like it here so much that you might just start dreaming of moving to the Welsh countryside, too.

tir bach farm

The Upside A pretty spot run by a seriously special couple. With climbing frames and farmyard animals (including 2 super-cute Shetland ponies called Cadog and Carreg) to amuse the kids, in countryside dotted with castles.

The Downside The fridge is a bit small.

The Facilities There are 20 tiered pitches, with 2 yurts in a further field, sleeping 6 and 4 respectively. The yurts have fixed kitchens plus utensils, a wood-burning stove, gas hob and water, but bring your own bedding. Balconies look out to the Preseli mountains. The lilac-painted shower block in the old milking parlour is spot-on, with 4 showers, including 2 big ones for washing kids. There's also a washing-up area with 2 big sinks, clothes-washing (£4–5) and drying facilities (£1 for 30 minutes), a shared fridge and freezer and mobile sockets. There's a communal fire pit at the bottom of the field.

Onsite Fun Children love the swings, slides, basketball court, badminton net and football area. Expect plenty of animal action. The farm's surrounded by mountains and 12 acres of ancient woodland with a small river running through it.

Offsite Fun Castell Henllys Iron Age Fort at Preseli hills (01239 891319; www.castellhenllys.com) is a 20-minute drive, with round houses constructed on original foundations. Scolton Manor (01437 731328; www.ilkcam.com) is just outside Haverfordwest. Llys-y-Fran reservoir (01437 532273) is great for fishing, boating, cycling and walking, and there's a café and play area. St David's is 45 minutes away, with plenty of history to keep everyone amused. The nearest beach is at Newport; kayaking and sailing at Cardigan Bay. There are other beaches less than an hour away, including Newgale (for watersports), Dinas Head (for cute little sandy beaches) and Newport Sands (for big sandy beaches).

If it Rains Onsite there's ping-pong next to some exciting farm machinery and a BBQ. There's a new heated swimming pool at Fishguard (01437 776639). You could easily spend a day touring the local castles, including Carew (01646 651782; www.carewcastle.com), Pembroke (01646 681510; www.pembroke-castle.co.uk) and Llawhaden (01443 336000).

Food & Drink The Old Post Office in Rosebush is good for home-made grub, including vegetarian and vegan options. Also try the traditional Welsh pub Tafarn Sinc (01437 532214) – good for meat-eaters. The Bont Pub at Llanglyden (01994 419575) does Sunday lunches. At Nevern there's the 16th-century Trewern Arms (01239 820395), which does decent food. For groceries try Bethesda farm shop and café, which sells excellent local meat, veg and bread.

Nanny State Alert There's a small river in the woodland at the bottom of the site. And don't get kicked by a milking cow either.

Getting There Turn right off the A40 onto the A478 and go through Llandissilio. Look out for the Bush Inn at the end of Llandissilio on the right-hand side. About a mile on look out for a left-hand turning signposted 'Llanycefn'. Follow until you come to a 5-road junction. Take the 3rd lane off this junction, keeping the yellow house to your right. Next look for a sign for 'Tir Bach' on a telegraph pole. Follow this lane until you see a thatched cottage on your left; Penhros Cottage. Tir Bach is opposite on the right.

Public Transport Pretty limited. The best option is to train it to nearby Clynderwen then take a taxi for the next 6 miles.

Open Easter–end Sept.

The Damage Adults £7 per night, children £3. Dogs allowed on a lead.

Tir Bach Farm Campsite, Llanycefn, Clynderwen, Pembrokeshire SA66 7XT

t 01437 532362   w www.tirbachfarm.co.uk   38 on the map

dale hill farm

Fresh sea air, family bonding, French cricket, flat lilos, frizzled sausages and stinky spilled milk in the cool bag. This is bargain-bucket camping, with a million-dollar view. High above Milford Haven estuary, you have a 180-degree vista before you. All for just a few squid.

Overlooking the mouth of the Pembrokeshire Heritage Coast is a simple field, where you and your kids (and, of course, anyone else who fancies it) can pitch your trusty canvas home-from-home and enjoy the simple pleasures of life – think of your kids roaming free in a lovely big field.

The farmers run a very relaxed ship and seem somewhat perplexed by campers' fascination with this field. After all, it is only a large field, backed by a rocky outcrop with a few grazing sheep – oh – and did we mention the view?

In high season it's a wetsuit-drying mecca, littered with surfboards and dinghies, smoking BBQs, impromptu ball games and kids ducking in and out of the guy ropes. Sheer magic.

Beware though; this site should really come with a warning – camping at Dale Hill Farm could induce a certain smugness. You could become smug because you are on the closest campsite to coveted Dale, with its surfy, yachty gang. Smug because you know that there's a shortcut from the back of the site to surf-tastic West Dale. And, finally, smug because you know that you have a field 'with a view' (unless, of course, the sea mist has rolled in).

dale hill farm

The Upside Stunning views; space by the bucket-load. Freedom.

The Downside Smugness may get the better of you.

The Facilities One huge field, where you can pitch wherever you want. It's best to set up your camp around the edge, so that everyone can roam free in the middle. The farmers are very chilled about what you can do here. One year, by request, they cut the grass into a cricket pitch. There's a functional amenities block just outside the field gate in the farmyard. It's no oil painting, but offers 2 showers, 2 loos and a washing-up room with a fridge-freezer. Queuing is unavoidable in high season. Charcoal BBQs are welcome, as is the family Fido, on a lead.

Onsite Fun Batting, balling and bicycling, tag and just hooning about. Younger kids enjoy playing in the Wendy house and sandpit.

Offsite Fun Crabbing on the pontoon is a compulsory pleasure (apparently it's bacon that gets them clinging on). Take a trip to the offshore island nature reserves of Skomer and Skokholm from the quay (01646 603110; www.dale-sailing.co.uk). Don't forget you're in the heart of the Pembrokeshire Heritage Coast (www.visitpembrokeshire.co.uk), with its array of stunning beaches and cliff walks. The area is popular with divers, too (07894 496824; www.divepembrokeshire.com).

If it Rains Wander across to the stunning bay of West Dale for some surfing/boogie-boarding. The local surf shop (01646 636642; www.surfdale.co.uk) offers lessons (and hires out all the latest gear) for surfing, windsurfing, kayaking, catamarans – if it floats they'll sort it. Folly Farm (01834 812731; www.folly-farm.co.uk) is one of those well-organised family-fun-day-type venues. Don't let this put you off, as it's actually perfect for a really soggy day – animals to stroke, a tour of the farm on a covered tractor-train, adventure playgrounds and a huge traditional funfair to round off the day.

Food & Drink The popular Griffin Inn (01646 636227) has kids coming out of its ears in high season – and is a great place for pub grub, or just to watch the comings and goings in the estuary. For teas, sandwiches and breakfasts, the café on the quay is good enough. There's a small shop in Dale for basics and hypermarkets in Haverfordwest. There are hopes to start a farm shop selling bread and milk-type basics.

Nanny State Alert The only rule here is no kite-flying due to the overhead cables. This is a working farm, so be tractor-beware.

Getting There As you enter the outskirts of Dale (on the B4327) you'll see ponds and marshland on your left. Go over the hump-backed bridge and shortly after take the right-hand turn. This is by the postbox and has a scruffy sign saying 'Dale Hill Farm'. Drive up the hill for about a mile and you'll come into the farmyard with the shower block in front of you.

Public Transport Take the train to Milford Haven then the Puffin Shuttle (coastal bus service no 315/400), which stops at the end of the road to the campsite. This takes about 20 minutes. Or take a taxi. During summer 2008 there was a pilot project running a boat taxi service from Milford Haven. Check to see if this is still going and book by calling Rudders Boatyard (01646 602681).

Open June–Oct, but worth ringing if you fancy visiting earlier.

The Damage A flat fee per night of £6 per tent.

Dale Hill Farm, Dale, Haverfordwest, Pembrokeshire SA62 3QX

t 01646 636359

39 on the map

trehenlliw farm

Beauty and the Beast? This back-to-basics site, where you're left to your own devices, is surely Beauty on a Budget, all set against a stunning backdrop of marshland and examples of North Pembrokeshire's finest mountains.

Some of the buildings at Trehenlliw are a bit tatty and the adventure playground is sort of overgrown, but this all seems to add to the character of the place. It's definitely a function-over-form kinda hangout – and that's what all the regulars love about it.

The large, flat camping field is cocooned within the 150 acres of farmland, which is mainly used for sheep and breeding cattle. There are no streetlights to pollute the night sky, so the strip of moor immediately behind the campsite is a wonderful place for your kids to watch for wildlife after dark, including fox cubs and barn owls.

The well-known local landmarks of mountains Carnllidi and Penberi frame the serenest of sunsets and also let you know that surf and sand central, aka Whitesands Bay, is only a mile or so away – so if everyone's clamouring for sand and sea, this is a good place to aim for.

St David's is only a quick 10-minute stroll away, though it can get pretty hectic during the summer months. So you'll find that Trehenlliw is not too far from the madding crowd, but far enough away to let you breathe easy in high season.

trehenlliw farm

The Upside No rules and regulations. Secluded, but convenient for beach and National Park life.

The Downside Despite this being a very basic campsite, it's really difficult to think of a downside. The twin B's: 'basic' and 'budget' are what the punters demand here.

The Facilities There isn't a set number of pitches. Once the area around the perimeter of the field is full, that's it, until someone moves off. For ablutions there are male and female shower blocks, with free hot water, situated away from the field, around the back of the farm buildings (so a potty might be a useful night-time accoutrement). Cleaning operates on a 'clean up after yourself' system, with detergents readily available. The outdoor washing-up sink and water tap are at the entrance to the camp field. There are 5 hoses and hook-ups available for camper vans and caravans.

Onsite Fun The freedom to enjoy the space in the centre of the camp field. Exploring one of the tracks through the farm or the overgrown playground. Stroking the horses and chatting to the chickens.

Offsite Fun The Pembrokeshire Coast National Park is on your doorstep in all its glory and with a mega choice of beaches. Learn to surf with the Ma Simes dudes (01437 720433; www.masimes.co.uk) at Whitesands, only 5 minutes' drive away. Families with older kids love the outdoor adventures, such as 'coasteering' (jumping off cliffs into freezing water) with TYF (01437 721611; www.tyf.com). You can also opt for boat trips around the nature reserve of Ramsey Island (01437 720285; www.ramseyisland. co.uk), or go seal-, whale- and dolphin-spotting.

If it Rains Culture vultures can do the galleries of St David's, then head for the cathedral and Bishop's Palace. The spanking-new leisure centre 7 miles away in Fishguard has 2 pools (one perfect for non-swimmers), a gym and sauna (01348 874514). The tiny independent cinema in Fishguard, Theatre Gwaun (01348 873421), has limited opening hours, but is worth a visit for the experience alone.

Food & Drink St David's has a deli, butcher, greengrocer and small well-stocked supermarket, CK's. If you shop with one of the big boys, drive 15 miles to Haverfordwest. There's also a yum-scrum country market in the tiny City Hall every Thursday morning. Think home-made pies, Welshcakes, *barabrith* (worth a nibble even if you haven't a clue what we're talking about). The city is fast becoming foodie heaven: Cwtch (01437 720491) serves modern classics in cool, friendly surroundings (with colouring-in bits to keep kids amused while they're waiting). Jones's café next door does a mean full Welsh. For local soup (cawl) head for the refectory at the cathedral and if you want a bog-standard take-away, the rugby club does this in high season.

Nanny State Alert This is a working farm, so be aware of vehicles in the yard. Otherwise your only concern could be sheep poo on your crocs.

Getting There Coming out of St David's on Nun Street (A487), take a left at the Rugby Club onto the B4583. Pass the left turn to Whitesands and shortly after you'll see a drive on the left. Go down here and into the farmyard.

Public Transport The nearest station is Haverfordwest, then take a bus to St David's, followed by a 10-minute walk. You can also get a bus from Fishguard to St David's. In the summer get the Coastal bus, which stops at the campsite gate.

Open Mid-April–end Oct.

The Damage In high season, the rates are about £10 for a family and £12 with hook-up.

Trehenlliw Farm, St David's, Haverfordwest, Pembrokeshire SA62 6PH

t 01437 721601

40 on the map

woodhouse farm

Want to 'get back to nature'? If you like the
sound of this, then the wild-flower fields of this site
are perfect places to make contact with the
natural world. And it's nice to be able to
sleep in a real tipi, too.

If your children are bookworms then they might well know that Rupert Bear often talks about the flower meadowsweet. So we think Rupert would have been very happy at Woodhouse Farm, a registered nature reserve, with meadowsweet growing in abundance, and the River Marteg running alongside it.

It's a pretty harmonious spot, surrounded by rolling upland pastures studded with caramel cattle and white fluffy sheep. And meadowsweet is only for starters: if you pitch your tent there in late spring or summer, the chances are you'll wake up in a field carpeted with wild flowers. Hay rattle, speedwell, forget-me-nots,

milkwort, red clover, white celandine, meadow buttercups, harebells and meadow vetch all burst forth in the camping field.

Most children love getting up close and personal with bugs, beetles and things that can swim, and so they can get stuck into pond-dipping among the bulrushes and giant golden king-cups, while you get stuck into a bottle of Chablis. You can keep an eye on the sunset at the same time.

Before you know it, you'll be bottling up meadowsweet wine to take home. Watch out though: Rupert Bear never let on, but it's potent stuff.

woodhouse farm

The Upside Heavenly camping in a mellow valley.

The Downside The facilities are limited. If the bunkhouse barn's booked to a single party, then there's just 1 chemical loo.

The Facilities There are no designated pitches, but you're unlikely to be squashed. There's a tipi with gas-burner and stove; charcoal's provided, but bring bedding. The bunkhouse sleeps 20. Facilities for campers are basic: showers and toilets in the bunkhouse are available to campers by arrangement, and if it's full then not at all. Basic chemical toilet tents are available, but you're advised to bring your own lav tent. There's a little onsite shop selling camping supplies and snacks.

Onsite Fun The place is run as a smallholding, with rare-breed pigs, sheep, ponies, ducks and chickens; children can help at feeding time. The river's good for swimming if the water's high. You can fish, as this is one of the best salmon rivers in the country. It's a great place for spotting wildlife, too, including otters, grasshoppers and 52 bird species.

Offsite Fun A network of tracks runs off the site for walking, cycling and horse-riding, and if you have older children the Glyndwr's Way long-distance path (01597 827562; www.nationaltrail.co.uk) and Gilfach Farm Nature Reserve (01597 870301; www.westwales.co.uk) are within walking distance. You can hire ponies at the Royal Lion Hotel (01597 810202; www.lionroyal.co.uk) in Rhayader. At the Gigrin Farm Red Kite Centre (01597 810243; www.gigrin.co.uk) red kites are fed every afternoon.

If it Rains Hereford's just over an hour away; there's plenty to explore around the cathedral, including the Chained Library (01432 374200; www.herefordcathedral.org) and the Mappa Mundi. Rhayader Leisure Centre (01597 810355/811013)

has a pool with supervised activities for children during the holidays and a kids' club on Mondays. Quackers Play Barn (01597 860111) at Newbridge-on-Wye should keep little children amused.

Food & Drink The Adams sell their own pork, bacon, lamb, eggs, bread and milk. They do home-cooked dinners (book the previous day). Packed lunches and breakfasts are also available. They hold BBQ weekends, and in September they host the Woodhouse Pork and Bacon Festival. There's a small health-food shop in Llanidloes beside the Cobbler's tea rooms (07973 782646). In Rhayader you can get a mean cream tea at Carole's tea rooms (01597 811060) and sublime fish and chips at Evan's Plaice (01597 810317).

Nanny State Alert The river along the edge of the site can flow very fast and quite deep in wet weather.

Getting There From Rhayader take the A470/A44 towards Llangurig for about 150 yards. On the right is Rhayader Leisure Centre and a turning signed B4518 to St Harmon. Take this road for 5 miles passing through St Harmon and on to Pant-y-Dwr. At the Mid Wales Inn turn right towards Bwylch-y-Sarnau. After a mile turn right just before a garage and continue for about half a mile. Woodhouse is on the right, signed with a finger post.

Public Transport The nearest train and bus stations are at Llandrindod Wells and Newtown, and a coach stops at Llanidloes. From Llandrindod there is a regular bus service to Rhayader and a limited service to St Harmon, but the owners collect from Llandrindod, Llanidloes or Newtown when they can.

Open All year, but call ahead in winter to check.

The Damage £2.50 per adult and £1.50 per child. Camping in field with no hook-up £7 for 2 adults (£10 with hook-up) and £2 per additional child.

Woodhouse Farm, St Harmon, Rhayader, Powys LD6 5LY

| t 01597 870081 | w www.woodhouse-farm.org.uk | 41 on the map |

gwerniago farm

Is it a pirate castle? Or a soldier's battalion? A fairy glen? Or a princess's tower? Don't tell the kids, but it's actually a rocky outcrop smack-bang in the middle of the camping field that they'll just love playing on. Making this the perfect place to dream a childhood dream.

What makes a perfect campsite? Quiet farmland location? Nearby beach? Friendly owners who like campfires, children and dogs?

Gwerniago Farm has all of the above and a lot more besides. Located in the pretty Dovey Valley, it's a large field, divided by the natural boundaries of a spreading oak and rocky outcrop. The family have farmed here for three generations now, so camping here gives you a great insight into a farmer's working life. Arrive at tea time and you might see farmer Trevor's sheepdog herding the cattle back out to their field, with Trevor opening gates ahead of them on his quad bike.

Little fire pits dot the site and the hustle and bustle of urban life seems a long way away; it'd be all too easy to spend several days here without feeling the need to leave the site at all.

But that might be a shame, as the beach and little harbour at Aberdyfi is less than a 15-minute drive north, and there's also Borth to the south. There's even a family-friendly pub in the village, within walking distance down a quiet lane.

You can't really ask for much more than that, can you?

gwerniago farm

The Upside Open space and lush valley; all you have to worry about is getting the kettle on.

The Downside Washing-up and shower facilities are a bit limited.

The Facilities The field's divided into 3 sections with masses of flat pitches, 3 with hook-ups. There's a facilities' block with 1 shower and 2 toilets each for gents and ladies. There's no sink, but campers can use one in reception. Internet is also available, and there are recycling bins and a fridge-freezer in the barn. The nearest launderette is 3 miles away in Machynlleth.

Onsite Fun Natural boundaries and mature trees provide plenty of excitement for children to explore and space to run around in. This is a working farm and children can watch the cows being milked. In the evenings Mair takes her ponies out for rides around the site (£2 a ride).

Offsite Fun Plenty of seaside activities at Borth, and the visitor centre there (01970 871174; www.visit-borth.co.uk) is staffed by friendly ladies. The pebbly beach is great when the weather's nice. It's a good spot for low-key surfing, and in summer there are lifeguards. Down the coast is Newquay (www.newquay-westwales.co.uk), with daily cruises to spot dolphins, harbour porpoises and grey Atlantic seals. North of Pennal, CAT (the Centre for Alternative Technology) (01654 705950; www.cat.org.uk) is popular with all ages. Grandma's Garden (01654 702244), with its arboretum, sculpture park and 'sight and light'/'scent and touch' gardens is worth a visit. There's an RSPB reserve at Eglwysfach, where you can see red kites and peregrine falcons.

If it Rains King Arthur's Labyrinth (01654 761584; www.kingarthurslabyrinth.com) at Corris Craft Centre is 15 minutes away and you can explore the myths of Arthur on a boat trip through the caverns. There's a leisure centre at Machynlleth (01654 703300; www.touristwales.co.uk) with a pool and slide. You can catch the train along the coast to Pwllheli (01758 613000; www.pwllheli.org.uk) from the town.

Food & Drink Try the homity pie at the CAT centre for a meal with a small carbon footprint, and if you're in Machynlleth their Quarry Café does local vegetarian food (01654 702624). There's a nice little coffee shop at Borth called Oriel Tir a Mor Gallery, which has a lovely upstairs room with squashy sofas if the weather is grim. Their cheese omelette makes a delicious lunch after a blustery walk on the beach. Buy dressed crabs a few doors up at Peter George, the butcher, who also does a mean line in home-made sausages.

Nanny State Alert The River Dovey, which runs near the site, can be very fast, and watch out for the tractors on the farm.

Getting There Turn right by the clock in Machynlleth, over the bridge, then immediately left. Follow that road for 2 miles on the Aberdyfi road. You will see a site sign on the left-hand side. Take that little road and the site is the first farm on the right.

Public Transport Take a train to Machynlleth (3 miles away from the site) then you can try taking an irregular bus, but it's probably better to jump in a taxi straight to the farm.

Open March–Nov.

The Damage £10 per couple, £5 per single person, £3 per teenager, £2 for children aged 4–12. Larger groups should ring in advance, and there's an additional £2 charge per night on bank holidays.

Gwerniago Farm Camping, Pennal, Machynlleth, Powys SY20 9JX

| t 01654 791227 | w www. gwerniago.co.uk | 42 on the map |

graig wen

The fields of tranquil Graig Wen are a pleasure to camp in, with the twitter and tweet of estuary birdlife as your soundtrack. But the big draw here is the disused railway line that runs right past the site and all the cycling escapades to be had along it.

The Mawddach Estuary is a hidden delight. It's concealed from casual onlookers by the dense vegetation between it and the main road through the area. But this place deserves to be discovered, and the best way to do this is to get onto the disused railway line that runs right along the side of the estuary, practically at water level. The track is now a walkway and cycle path that links the appealing old town of Dolgellau and the brash and breezy seaside resort of Barmouth.

From the track, you'll be able to witness this untouched, nature-filled place – a wonderful waterway that changes as the tide rises and falls. Graig Wen campsite fronts onto this track and the estuary itself, so this is a perfect spot to bring the tent, the kids and the bikes to. You can cycle all the way to Barmouth (which includes crossing the mouth of the estuary on a stunning bridge) without even seeing a road, and virtually the entire route to Dolgellau in the other direction is road-free, too.

Back at camp after a hard day's cycling, it's time to light a campfire, and after burning rubber all day, burning a few marshmallows on sticks seems like an extremely well-earned treat.

graig wen

The Upside Lots of space, lots of nature, and safe cycling right on your doorstep.

The Downside Can be a long trek to the facilities, depending on where you're pitched.

The Facilities There is a small touring site near the entrance with fantastic estuary views and space for up to 10 camper vans, small caravans or tents. This is a good spot for smaller kids, as this is where the toilet block is; 2 basic unisex showers are also available. A small shop sells marshmallows, citronella candles, eggs, milk, and the like. A track leads down the hill to around 40 acres of paddock and woodland, around which another 20 pitches are spread. This area is wild and unspoilt, and although there isn't much flat ground, it's a great location and campfires are allowed. Logs are available at the shop (£5). The only facility on hand in the lower section is one composting toilet. The field nearest the estuary is car-free; wheelbarrows are available for luggage.

Onsite Fun Test your animal-spotting skills – owls, nightjars, glow-worms, badgers and kingfishers are all in residence here. There are a couple of rope-swings, plenty of trees to climb, occasional wildlife walks and bikes to hire.

Offsite Fun In addition to the cycle track along the estuary, there's another family cycling path, plus a more challenging mountain-bike run, at nearby Coed-y-Brenin, around 5 miles north of Dolgellau.

If it Rains Back in Dolgellau, the interactive National Centre for Welsh Folk Music, better known as Ty Siamas (01341 421800; www.tysiamas.com), has an array of traditional Welsh instruments, which the kids can have a go at playing. There are also occasional live music nights. For something more theme park-like, King Arthur's Labyrinth (on the A487 between Dolgellau and Machynlleth (01654 761584; www.kingarthurslabyrinth.com) is an attraction themed around ancient myths and legends.

Food & Drink Stock up on local produce and tasty treats at the Country Market on Thursday mornings, or the Farmer's Market on the third Sunday of every month, both in Dolgellau. Down at Fairbourne, the unassuming Café Indiana is a pleasant surprise. South Indian specialities are created with colour and flourish from fresh ingredients and traditional home recipes. Plenty of non-spicy options available.

Nanny State Alert No fencing along the waterway. There are some steep wooded slopes onsite, too.

Getting There Graig-Wen is between Dolgellau and Fairbourne on the A493. From Dolgellau, the site is about 5 miles along the road, and is well signposted.

Public Transport The owners operate a pick-up service from the station at Morfa Mawddach, with a small charge for petrol. Trains run from Birmingham and Shrewsbury.

Open The touring site is open early March–early Jan; the lower field and yurts are currently only open for pre-bookings in summer school holidays, but this may be extended if planning permission is granted. Call ahead to check.

The Damage £18 per night for a family of 4. Under-5s go free, and there are reduced rates for cyclists and backpackers. A hook-up costs £2.85 per night. Well-behaved dogs on leads are welcome. Yurts £100–120 for 2 nights, depending on season. To maintain the appeal of this quiet and natural campsite, numbers are strictly limited, so pre-booking is essential.

Graig Wen, Arthog, Nr Dolgellau, Gwynedd LL39 1BQ

| t 01341 250482 | w www.graigwen.co.uk | 43 on the map |

shell island

This 45-acre peninsula of sand dunes and grass
on Snowdonia's coast is reserved just for campers.
And with a huge sandy beach just over the
dunes from your tent, the kids will never
run short of fun and games.

Sand dunes are great. Not only do they shield campers from bracing weather, they're also multi-functional playthings. You can run up them, cartwheel, jump or roll down them, build sandcastles on them, throw airplanes off them and fly kites from them. They embody the whole spirit of beachside camping in one neat lump of sand and tufty grass, and nowhere on Britain's coast has better dunes to camp amongst than Shell Island.

The beauty of Shell Island is that it's a remote, self-contained camping community, cut off from the rest of world save for a two-mile causeway. Admittedly, the arrivals area can be a bit of a shock at peak times. You may find a seething mass of humanity spilling out from the reception, pub, shops and café, but once you're through the barrier, the site opens up before you against a backdrop of clear blue seas, and it's down to you to find your own special slice of peninsula paradise.

Choose from cliff-top spots with great views, sheltered fields close to the amenities or small pockets of space around the dunes. There are a few pitches right on the sea at shore level, or secluded spots in the woods at the back of the peninsula. But wherever you choose, you're never far from that fantastic beach and all the fun of the dunes.

shell island

The Upside Remote, island-style family camping with a big bang of beach for your buck.

The Downside It's a popular place, so despite its huge size you'll have to work hard to find a quiet pitch at peak times.

The Facilities Lots! At the bustling reception area you'll find a supermarket, camping/beach shop, snack bar, restaurant, pub, free hot showers and laundry. Once you're out into the campsite proper, there are just a few portaloo-type toilets scattered around the place.

Onsite Fun The huge sand dunes and expansive beach are all you really need for daytime entertainment; campfires will provide the evening fun. During high season there is often some organised entertainment of the disco/karaoke variety back at the restaurant, but it's no contest for the draw of the campfire.

Offsite Fun Three miles north of Llanbedr is the town of Harlech, whose principal feature is a precariously perched castle, but whose narrow, winding streets are also worth exploring. The views of Cardigan Bay and the Snowdonia mountains make this town a great place to get your regional bearings; and once you have those, it would be rude not to go for at least a quick stroll somewhere in Snowdonia National Park (www.snowdonia-npa.gov.uk). For traditional British seaside resort attractions, head south along the coast to Barmouth, some 7 miles south of Shell Island causeway.

If it Rains It's only 3 miles to Harlech Castle (01766 780552; www.harlech.com), an impressive, well-preserved 13th-century fortress and a World Heritage Site. A family ticket for 2 adults and up to 3 kids is just £10.70. There's a shop just outside selling souvenirs and tongue-tingling ice creams. And if it keeps raining, Harlech also has a leisure centre (Ffordd-y-Traeth, Harlech; 01766 780576) with a swimming pool and badminton courts.

Food & Drink The onsite bar is brash and noisy. For something more subdued, the Victoria Inn (01341 241213; www.vic-inn.co.uk) back in Llanbedr is fashioned out of Welsh stone, has a steadfastly traditional interior and pretty family beer garden. Bar food is served daily. It's almost opposite the entrance to the causeway back on the mainland. For top-notch BBQ food, including delicious minted Welsh spring lamb kebabs, head to Dylan Richards Family Butcher, also in Llanbedr, located just over the causeway.

Nanny State Alert It's a huge site, so expect the kids to run off and get lost somewhere. Issuing them with a walkie-talkie might be helpful.

Getting There From Barmouth, take the A496 north towards Harlech. At Llanbedr village, turn left at the bridge and follow the road to the causeway.

Public Transport If you're on public transport, Llanbedr railway station on the Cambrian Coast line is on the mainland side of the causeway. It's a couple of miles' walk from there, but will feel longer with kids and heavy gear.

Open March–Oct.

The Damage A family of 4 costs £17 in low season and £20 in high season. Dogs £2. Weekly rates available. There's a minimum 3 nights on Whitsun and August Bank Holiday. Tents and motor homes only, no caravans.

Shell Island, Llanbedr, Merioneth, Gwynedd LL45 2PJ

| t 01341 241453 | w www.shellisland.co.uk | 44 on the map |

the green caravan park

Dare to camp deep in rural Shropshire with
Ronnie and Reggie and *The Sopranos*? Fear not.
Twin pygmy goats and rare Soprano Pipistrelle
bats are just some of the other residents at this
eco-friendly site.

Site owner Karen Donohue's family has been running this campsite for 21 years, and she has seen many families return year after year. She reckons it's the magnetic effect of the river (particularly on the kids) that keeps 'em coming back.

The site sits in the Onny Valley, with the River East Onny running through it. Shallow enough for paddling and catching tiddlers (don't worry if you didn't bring a net – the shop will be happy to sell one to you), the river is also great for playing Pooh Sticks from the little bridges. And the local wildlife likes it here, too. There are 32 bird boxes along the river and 59 species of bird have been recorded by campers. Bat boxes, a wild area, recycling facilities and energy-efficient lighting have also helped the site to gain a David Bellamy Gold Conservation award for good environmental practices and commitment to preserving the natural world.

The site has a friendly and relaxed atmosphere, and Karen tries to keep it a fairly rule-free zone, but she does have three: keep to the five-miles-an-hour speed limit, keep your doggy friend on a lead and be sure to clear up after him, too. Well, four if you count the quiet zone from 10pm to 8am.

the green caravan park

The Upside Simple ppp-pleasures by the riverside – Pooh Sticks, paddling and picnicking.

The Downside There are lots of caravans as well as tents here – as you might guess by the site name.

The Facilities Three main camping areas – a rally field, hook-up area and a tent field without hook-ups. But there are also a few little camping nooks and crannies. The 'island' has 11 pitches (restricted to camping couples in busy periods), and there are several 'dingles' – small grassy areas next to the river, surrounded by trees. The fairly large facilities block in the middle of the site has 10 women's toilets and 2 hand basins in one room, and 5 showers (20p coin op) and another 6 hand basins in the other, and the same for men. There are 5 washing-up sinks, a washing machine and tumble-dryer, and an information notice board. The shop is open 9am–6pm at weekends, and subject to demand at other times. It sells basic provisions, small toys, fishing nets and bits and pieces like tent pegs and tea towels. A small charge (for charity) is made for freezing icepacks or charging mobiles.

Onsite Fun A playground, the river for paddling and catching tiddlers, plenty of space for family games and even pygmy goats to take for a walk.

Offsite Fun This is great walking country. The Offa's Dyke National Trail runs close by, and the Onny Valley lies between the heather-clad Long Mynd and the craggy outcrops of the Stiperstones Ridge. But don't tell the children that! Of course we are not just going for a walk up that big hill – we are hunter-gatherers foraging for wimberries.

If it Rains Head into the bohemian, colourful, higgledy-piggledy Bishops Castle. As well as its 2 small museums: the House on Crutches Museum (01588 630007) is supported by wooden posts over a cobbled alley and the Bishops Castle Railway and Transport Museum (01588 638446), you can browse its eclectic mix of shops, including the Yarborough House second-hand book and record shop, which also has a coffee shop (01588 638318; www. yarboroughhouse.com).

Food & Drink If you don't fancy the Inn on the Green (01588 650105; www.theinnonthegreen.net), which is right next door to the campsite, a short, steep walk up the hill brings you to the Crown Inn in Wentnor (01588 650613), which has real ales, roasts, baguettes and a children's menu. Bishops Castle has lots of eateries, with children welcome at the own-brew Three Tuns (01588 638797) and the (also own-brew) Six Bells (01588 630144).

Nanny State Alert Most of the river is shallow enough for paddling in, but watch out for some deeper areas.

Getting There From the A49, turn onto the A489 and follow the brown signs onto the A488 to the site. From the A483, turn onto the A498 and again follow the brown signs.

Public Transport It's a bit off the beaten track so public transport options are limited. However, Shropshire Shuttle Buses (www.shropshirehillsshuttles.co.uk) from Shrewsbury stop outside the Inn on the Green 3 times a day at weekends and Bank Holiday Mondays.

Open March–Oct.

The Damage A tent with 2 adults and 2 children costs £14 a night (plus £2 to charity if you want to stay past check-out time).

The Green Caravan Park, Wentnor, Bishops Castle, Shropshire SY9 5EF

| t | 01588 650605 | w | www.greencaravanpark.co.uk | 45 | on the map |

barn farm

Plenty for kids to do here – they can get a good look at some farm animals, spot wildlife and hear spooky stories about witches and wizards. Adults can admire a great view, a pretty village and nosh good pub grub, right on the doorstep.

Camping at Barn Farm started when a lone caravaner asked Gilbert if he could park up on his traditional Derbyshire gritstone stock farm, in this beautiful part of the Peak District. Twenty years on, Barn Farm is a popular, relaxed camping spot for families and school groups, as well as ramblers, who can head off on the footpaths that lead directly from the site.

The site sits just below mystical Stanton Moor, with its prehistoric Nine Ladies Stone Circle. More recent legend has it that nine dancing ladies and a fiddler were turned to stone for frolicking on the Sabbath! Kids will love the resident water buffaloes, peacocks, free-range chickens and cattle, and there's a good chance of spotting some of the farm's other furry and feathered residents – wildlife visitors include badgers and black fallow deer, as well as nuthatches, dippers and peregrine falcons. And don't tell the kids you're going for an evening stroll across Stanton Moor – 'we're going on a bat hunt' is so much more exciting!

On the edge of the pretty village of Birchover, the two main sloping camping fields have wonderful views over the Derwent Valley, and if things get a bit busy, the campsite opens up other fields, so you should still be able to find yourself a nice peaceful spot.

barn farm

The Upside Space, and plenty of it, with acres of farmland, lovely views and onsite animals. Haven for wildlife, including badgers, rare black fallow deer and over 60 species of birds.

The Downside A little on the pricey side and showers are (eek!) school-PE-changing-room style. Like most campsites it can get a bit noisy on a busy weekend night – although the owners have a 'no noise after 10.30pm' policy.

The Facilities Unmarked pitches are spread out over several fields – there are 200 acres of farmland available. The funky main toilet and shower block has Barbie Pink for girls and Tangerine Orange for boys. No nappy-changing facilities, but there are 2 roomy disabled-access toilets with showers. There are further toilet blocks around the site, as well as washing-up facilities, a washing machine, tumble-dryer, hairdryers and even a sauna.

Onsite Fun No formal playground, but plenty of trees to climb and a rope-swing with a great view over the fields and valley – plus fields for the kids to kick their heels in and roam.

Offsite Fun The walk across Stanton Moor to Nine Ladies is a pleasant stroll and can be turned into a bat walk in the evening. Just off the moor a footpath takes you through an eco-warrior camp, where you can see a bit of extreme camping – tunnels and tree houses were used here to protest against a potential new development.

If it Rains Games galore in the games room, including table football, air hockey, table tennis and pool. The curious seaside-resort-style Matlock Bath is only 3 miles away, with treats on offer including the cable-car ride to the Heights of Abraham (01629 582365; www.heightsofabraham.com) open daily during camping season 10am–5pm; cost £10.50 adults and £7.50 children (under-5s go free). Here you can explore underground caverns, find out about lead-miners and enjoy the view from the wooded hillside and the adventure playground.

Food & Drink Birchover is surprisingly well endowed for food and drink. Two good pubs are within easy walking distance of the campsite and both welcome children: the more traditional Red Lion Inn (01629 650363), and the upmarket gastro-pub Druid Inn (01629 650302). Book in advance for weekend evenings during the walking season. The friendly village shop is open 7am–7pm and sells all the basics.

Nanny State Alert Barn Farm is a working farm with all the usual agricultural machinery and 'muck' around.

Getting There From the A6 take the B5056 until you see the sign for Birchover on the right. Go through the village and Barn Farm is signposted on the right after the last houses.

Public Transport The 172 bus runs to Matlock and Bakewell and stops about 10 minutes' walk from the site in the middle of the village.

Open March–Oct.

The Damage £7.50 per adult and £3.75 for kids under 7. Dogs are not encouraged, but ask nicely and they can come free with permission as long as you keep them on the lead. No male- or female-only groups allowed. Several camping barns, sleeping up to 15 people, are also available from £100 per night.

Barn Farm, Birchover, Matlock, Derbyshire DE4 2BL

t   01629 650245/07977 426221

46   on the map

haddon grove

What's the really essential ingredient for successful camping with kids? More kids, of course! This site is likely to have plenty of them – so your juniors will be able to keep themselves occupied without your help, allowing you to sit back and relax.

With plenty of room for the kids to roam, this back-to-basics camping on a family-only field has great views thrown in. A short walk downhill and you're by the river, with its small weirs and shallow pools for splashing in. As long as they've got space to run around in, the kids probably won't need much more than this. And it's a pretty safe bet that there'll be plenty of playmates on hand.

The field has lots of room for ball games, and the small wooded area separating the family field from its neighbour is good for hide-and-seek. A rope-tyre swing hanging from a tree completes the low-key play facilities.

Although the kids probably won't appreciate this, you are pitched just a couple of fields away from the spectacular limestone gorge of Lathkill Dale – the far end of the field has the best views. What they probably will appreciate is that the site is a short (although steep) walk from the river, where the series of weirs and pools make great wet-play areas.

This area is also a haven for wildlife – Lathkill Dale is one of the five valleys making up the Derbyshire Dales National Nature Reserve. Look out for dippers hopping in and out of the river, and see how many different kinds of butterfly you can spot.

haddon grove

The Upside Cheap and cheerful, back-to-basics camping in a family field with the river only a short walk away.

The Downside The family-only field is furthest from the toilets, so it's a bit of a trek. The nearest pubs are 2 miles away and shops are 4 miles away – so come prepared for this.

The Facilities Unmarked pitches are spread over 3 fields, although one of these is mainly for caravans. The best place for camping with kids is the family-only field at the far end of the site, although some groups of families choose the larger field, for groups. The toilet and shower block are pretty basic (it's a working sheep farm) with 5 toilets and 2 showers in the women's block, and 1 shower and 4 toilets in the men's. Both have washing-up areas, and there's a family shower room. Although there is no shop, David (the farmer) will usually find you some milk and teabags as he directs you back into Bakewell, where you can stock up on provisions. He can re-freeze icepacks.

Onsite Fun Playing family games, hiding-and-seeking in the wood, and hanging out with all the other kids.

Offsite Fun A short, but sometimes steep and rocky, path walk takes you down to Lathkill Dale, where you take a left along the river to reach the first of a number of small weirs and shallow pools; perfect for paddling and splashing around in.

If it Rains The 12th-century medieval manor house, Haddon Hall (01629 812855; www.haddonhall.co.uk) is a 15-minute drive away, while the home of the Duke and Duchess of Devonshire, Chatsworth House (01246 565300; www.chatsworth.org), can be reached in less than half an hour by car.

Food & Drink Two good pubs are about 2 miles in either direction. Traditional pub food can be had at the Bull's Head (01629 812372) in Monyash, which is right next door to the village green and (more importantly) the excellent village playground, which caters for tots to teens and even has equipment adapted for kids with special needs. In the opposite direction, the Lathkil Hotel at Over Haddon (01629 812501; www.lathkil.co.uk) has food with a view, including yummy puds.

Nanny State Alert The ponies around the farm aren't for petting or feeding.

Getting There From Bakewell, take the B5055 towards Monyash and after about 3 miles turn left onto a long narrow lane, which is signposted 'Haddon Grove'. You'll find the campsite at the bottom of the lane. Travelling from Buxton, take the A515 and turn left onto the B5055. Go through Monyash, and the lane to Haddon Grove is on your right after about 2 miles.

Public Transport Trent Barton Transpeak buses (01773 712265; www.trentbarton.co.uk) run to Bakewell from Nottingham, Derby and Manchester (there's also a 6.1 from Derby) and First South Yorkshire buses (0871 200 2233; www.firstgroup.com) operate between Sheffield and Bakewell. The 177 bus runs between Bakewell and Monyash 5 times a day.

Open March–Oct.

The Damage A family tent, including the campers, is a bargain at £7.50 a night.

Haddon Grove Caravan and Campsite, Haddon Grove Farm, Bakewell, Derbyshire DE45 1JF

t 01629 812343

47 on the map

rowter farm

Ah – the highs and lows of camping! Spend the
morning watching paragliders circling gracefully around
Mam Tor summit, then descend through the ravine
of Winnats Pass for an afternoon's exploration of
underground caves.

If you and your brood are active, outdoorsy types, and your kids enjoy nothing better than a good brisk walk scrambling up and down hills and rocks, then Rowter Farm deserves a visit. A short walk from the site takes you past Windy Knoll Cave, where prehistoric bones from wolves, bison, bears, hares and reindeer were discovered, to the summit of Mam Tor (or Mother Hill), once the home to ancient Celtic tribes.

To give you some idea of the wonderful sense of space here, site owner Sarah Mark grew up on Rowter Farm and finds the wide-open landscapes of nearby Edale a bit 'claustrophobic'! The farm sits at the head of the Hope Valley, some 230 metres above sea level, and just above the spectacularly steep-sided Winnats Pass.

The best time to visit the farm is during the early summer, when the children can enjoy some country sights and sounds – sheep being rounded up for shearing, lambs frolicking in nearby fields and swallows swooping in and out of the farm buildings. The chickens scratching around the farmyard and goats and cows in the fields can be seen all season.

Given the ups and downs of camping, Rowter Farm should be high on anyone's list.

rowter farm

The Upside Wonderful sense of space, but if you're feeling a bit too far from the madding crowd, bustling Castleton is just down the road. Relaxed policy as to when you leave.

The Downside As it's high up, it can be exposed – Winnats does mean 'wind gates'. Like other sites in the Peak District that take groups, it can get noisy on a busy Saturday night – although Sarah tries to enforce a no-late-night noise policy.

The Facilities The site has unmarked pitches and can take up to 5 caravans and about 40 tents, although it only gets really busy on Bank Holiday weekends. The facilities are basic, with a dish-washing room, 2 women's and 1 men's toilet, hand basins, and 2 showers (50p). The small shop is usually open from 8am to 9pm and sells eggs, long-life milk, chocolate and bread. It also has matches and disposable BBQs (which are allowed, although campfires are banned). Dogs are welcome.

Onsite Fun While Sarah thinks 'there's not much here for kids', growing up on a farm means you tend to take farm animals and wide-open spaces for granted. The middle of the camping field (tents mainly pitch around the edge) is perfect for family games of French cricket, football and rounders.

Offsite Fun Mam Tor – which has superb views over the Hope Valley – is a short walk with kids, while a longer walk along the Limestone Way takes you into Castleton. There, Peveril Castle (01433 620613; www.english-heritage.org.uk), perched high above the town, has what English Heritage calls 'breathtaking' views over the Peak District.

If it Rains With 10 miles of underground caves below the Castleton area, you're spoilt for choice. Take an underground boat trip in Speedwell Cavern (01433 620512; www.speedwellcavern.co.uk),

snigger at the name of the largest natural cave entrance at the Peak Cavern (www.devilsarse.com), visit the home of the semi-precious Blue John stone at Blue John Cavern (01433 620638; www.bluejohn-cavern.co.uk) or explore Treak Cliff Cavern (01433 620571).

Food & Drink The site is quite a long walk from the nearest pub, but there are plenty of pubs in Castleton serving food. Children are welcome at the Bull's Head (01433 620256; www.bullsheadcastleton.co.uk), Castle Hotel (01433 620578) and the George (01433 620238; www.georgehotelcastleton.co.uk).

Nanny State Alert No particular hazards, although it's a working farm, with plenty of machinery and farm vehicles.

Getting There The site can be difficult to find as the sign on the gate from the road is very small. Travelling from Sparrow Pit towards Castleton on the A6187, there is a metal gate leading to the track to the site on the right, just before you reach a fork in the road. If you start to go down into Winnats Pass and see signs to the caves, you've gone too far. Turn back round and look out for the gate on your left.

Public Transport It's a tricky journey by public transport as the 173 bus, which runs near by, only operates on Sundays and Bank Holidays. The nearest railway station is at Hope, and although the 272 bus takes you to Castleton, taxis from there are few and far between.

Open Easter–Oct.

The Damage Prices per night are: £5 adults, £2 children (under 12s), £3 children aged between 12 and 16.

Rowter Farm, Castleton, Hope Valley, Derbyshire S33 8WA

t   01433 620271

48 on the map

family festivals

If you love festivals, maybe your kids will too. Spend carefree summer days with them, dancing in a faraway field.

If you've picked up this book for research purposes, then your idea of an all-nighter has no doubt changed a bit over the years. Calpol and cocoa are probably the strongest things you want to get your hands on these days, but that doesn't mean that you have to hang up your dancing shoes altogether.

Let's face it, no one knows how to throw a party quite like we do, and the explosion of festivals across the country is colourful proof of the fact that becoming a parent – or even a grandparent – doesn't mean throwing in the party towel just yet. Of course, there are some parties that are best just left to the grown-ups. While it might not be that appropriate to take kids to a techno-festival like Glade, there are plenty of family-friendly festivals that have become as essential a part of the English summer as school sports day or strawberries and cream.

The fact that Glastonbury has not sold out recently suggests that punters are increasingly eschewing the big commercial events, with their onsite cashpoint machines and mobile-phone charging stations, for something a bit more hand-made and authentic. The festivals on the following pages are great places to take your children for a weekend of fun, whether they are babes-in-arms, tots, in-betweeners or sulky teens.

camp bestival

Baby sibling to Bestival on the Isle of Wight in September, Camp Bestival takes place at Lulworth Castle against the backdrop of the Jurassic Coast in Dorset. A quirky retro feel characterises this festival, which is really dominated by children. This is one for the family, and the kids' field is fantastic, with an insect circus, Maypole, Punch and Judy and endless activities. Breastival Mother and Baby Temple means that even the youngest family members needn't be left at home. The onsite farmer's market means that you never have to stray too far away from your comfort zone as there's good-quality food on offer.

Lulworth Castle, Dorset; 08448 884410 (ticketline); www.ticketline.co.uk or www.campbestival.co.uk; mid–July.

the larmer tree

Originally the site of a Victorian theme park in Cranbourne Chase, Dorset, Larmer Tree is opened every year by Jools Holland and in 2008 it won the Family Festival Award. It has a maximum capacity of 5,000, and there isn't a scrap of corporate sponsorship in sight, which is just as we like it. Dressing up is an essential part of the fun, so children love it, and there are usually at least five stages with a thumping selection of folk, roots, blues, jazz, reggae and country music. Something for everyone, with a finale on Sunday night, where festival-goers, especially kids, parade in costumes they've made over the weekend.

PO Box 1790, Salisbury SP5 5WA; 01725 552300; www.larmertreefestival.co.uk; mid-July.

shambala

There are whispers that Shambala is the festival expert's festival and has maintained the sort of laid-back vibe that was what all festivals used to be like before cashpoints, photo ID and monumental barriers spoiled all the fun. It's been going for a decade, moving from Bristol, where it started, to Northamptonshire, and there are few, if any, other festivals that have such a strong sense of community. Festivals with kids can be a bit fraught, but at Shambala you almost feel you could let your toddler toddle off for a dance on his own, and some kind girl dressed as a fairy would bring him back to you (probably not wise to rely on this, though!).

Northamptonshire; www.shambalafestival.org; last Bank Holiday in August.

guilfest

Having won the Family Festival Award in 2006, Guilfest has paid its dues in terms of laying on a great musical line-up combined with circus tents, play areas, workshops and theatre clubs to entertain the children. As well as a fabulous family area, the festival is packed with street theatre acts, including a Space Age children's carnival, who wander through the site. The Kidzone team, who have been coming to the festival for years and also work at other festivals, are great at laying on activities your children will love, in particular the children's talent parades, fairground rides and all the usual acrobatics workshops, which make this a really special festival for a family outing.

Guildford, Surrey; 01483 454159 (for more information); tickets available on door and from Ticketline; mid-July.

dorset steam fair

Now, we know that this might seem slightly esoteric, but we are hoping you will trust us that this festival is possibly the highlight of the summer-party calendar for familes who like festivals and love camping. It has the charm of an old-fashioned fairground, with showman's wagons, two gorgeous carousels and lots of 19th-century steam locomotives, combined with a splash of glamour in the form of dancing girls and fortune-tellers, and with heavy horses, military vehicles, a sheep show, farming exhibition and lashings of first-rate food stalls thrown in for good measure, too. There is also a musical line-up that should make some of the more established 'music festivals' feel ashamed.

Dairy House Farm, Child Okeford, Blandford, Dorset DT11 8HT; 01258 860361; early Sept.

wood festival

Wood is an affirmation of life, love and family; everything that's best about a home-made festival. It's a cosy event, with a largely acoustic line-up. It defines eco-chic, with showers heated by wood-burning stoves and a solar-powered main stage (the loos are, of course, composting). There are family workshops to keep your tribe happy plus there's a smell of woodsmoke in the air and girls wear real flowers in their hair as children tumble among haybales. At Wood, there is some of the original spirit of Woodstock. Just on a very, very small scale.

Braziers Park, Oxfordshire OX10 6AN; 01235 821262; www.thisistruck.com; mid-May.

la rosa

Prepare yourself for a real treat: psychedelic vintage caravans, a smiling Buddha and Tutankhamun in the trees as well as some pretty colourful kitsch – with the Yorkshire Dales and the salty delights of Whitby just a heartbeat away. In four words, heaven in a caravan.

If Gypsy Rose Lee had got at the magic mushrooms then La Rosa is the site she would have created. You might well miss the bunch of red plastic roses on the gate that mark the bumpy track down to the site, and this is part of what makes arriving there a treat. It's like finding a diamond in the middle of a muddy field.

Each wagon is decorated according to a different theme, so if you fancy a safari night, an Elvis evening or even a psycho-candy afternoon, then you'll find a wagon that will push your buttons. Plus you'll discover a tipi to chill out in and a woodland for children to explore, too.

It's surely not surprising that children love the sense of playfulness that dances through this site: and you'll find that it's almost impossible to be in a bad mood here.

And when you've tired of the multicolour thrills of your caravan, the emerald-green delights of the Yorkshire Dales are on your doorstep. You can even catch a train all the way to Goathland and walk to the site; it's quite right, too, that the steam train chugging past the site every few hours is Harry Potter's very own Hogwart's Express. You didn't really think that it would just be an ordinary train, now, did you?

la rosa

The Upside Luxurious yurt and tipi accommodation. Children will love exploring the site, with its endless secret hiding places and den-making opportunities. The caravans are pretty awesome, too.

The Downside You will have to carry your water up to the top field.

The Facilities Divided between a lower field with 4 caravans, all with stoves, and a larger top field with another 5 caravans, and slightly more basic facilities. The lower field is nearer the water supply, but the top field is great for a group, and there's a communal big top stuffed with fifties' tea sets, dressing-up clothes and games. None of the caravans has electricity, but candles are provided. Both fields have a fire pit, but the top field has a chilling-out tipi, too. Showers are in the old milking parlour, and there's a shepherd's hut with a composting loo dressed up as a gypsy wagon. Bedding and fuel are provided.

Onsite Fun Aspiring Stepford Wives will love the vintage tea sets in the big top, and the possibility they offer for creating a Valium-fuelled tea party.

Offsite Fun Goths in long leather coats swoop around Whitby like bats, where the legend of Dracula whispers through the little streets. It's a good place for a day out and the harbour's a great site for crabbing. Get your bait from Catch of the Day on Pier Road. Book a boat trip with Cooks Endeavour Cruise Trips (07813 781034; www.endeavourwhitby.com) or Angling Party Pontoons for fishing trips (01947 605658). At Esk Leisure (01947 820550; www.whitbyonline.co.uk), Ruswarp, there's crazy golf, and also a surprisingly good café. Farsyde Stud and Riding Centre (01947 880249) is the best place for riding, especially on the beach and across the moor. Hire cycles at Trailways (01947 820207; www.trailways.fsnet.co.uk).

If it Rains The Whitby Museum (01947 602908; www.whitbymuseum.org.uk) has some good pirate displays. Look out, in particular, for the severed hand. There's also a leisure centre in Whitby. Moors National Park Centre (01439 772737; www.visitnorthyorkshiremoors.co.uk) has a climbing cave as well as good displays about local wildlife. If you have teenagers or older children, take them to the Dracula Experience (01947 601923; www.draculaexperience.co.uk).

Food & Drink The fish at the Whitby Catch on Pier Road is great. Magpie's restaurant (01947 602058) is top-notch, but its success is reflected in the queues. Children will probably prefer to buy fish and chips from their take-away and eat them on the pier. On a cold day the huge hot chocolates at Sherlock's (01947 603399) are a sugary treat. For a traditional tea room pop into Bothams (01947 602 823; www.botham.co.uk), where you can also buy all you need for a picnic.

Nanny State Alert You can use candle s in your caravans – just be very, very careful.

Getting There Take the A64, then the 169 to Pickering. In Goathland, follow the Egton Bridge Roman Road for just over 2 miles, then turn right. You'll see red plastic flowers on the gatepost after you turn. Follow the track to the bottom of the hill.

Public Transport Catch a train or bus to Whitby, where buses run to Goathland. Use your legs for the rest of the way – along a footpath, then a 20-minute walk through woods. For directions call the site.

Open April–Sept.

The Damage £27 per person per night, including bedding, gas, candles and firewood. July and August 2 nights minimum. Under-5s free. No dogs allowed.

La Rosa Campsite Extraordinaire, Murk Esk Cottage, Goathland, Whitby, North Yorkshire YO22 5AS

| t | 07786 072866 | w | www.larosa.co.uk | 49 | on the map |

spiers house

Deep in the forest, the children eventually came
to a clearing with ... no, not a gingerbread house, but
a big campsite with a playground, ranger activities and
bike tracks galore. Don't forget to sprinkle breadcrumbs if
you want to find your way back.

Nearly a mile from the nearest road and surrounded by Cropton Forest, the site has a remote, almost magical, feel about it. Swathes of uncut areas of wild grasses and flowers and lines of trees throughout the site help to maintain a tranquil air, despite its size. During the day, when many families have headed off to the nearby coast and surrounding area, pheasants stroll around the site as though they own it.

Kids' bikes are a must here, with gravel paths for tootling around the site, and way-marked cycle paths leading off the site for exploring the forest by pedal-power. (If you forget to pack your bikes, hire them at the Forestry Commission Keldy site, a 35-minute walk or a 10-minute car ride up the road through Cropton.) As well as the shady adventure playground, which provides a focal point, a stream running down the side of the site is great for dipping and paddling. And rangers run nature activities to help kids discover forest secrets – such as deer-stalking, nightjar-searching and early-bird walks.

Camping purists may object to the 40 forest lodges around the perimeter of the site, but this will extend the 'camping' season – and appeal to less-hardy families!

spiers house

The Upside Camping in a peaceful, woodland playground with the added bonus of organised activities on hand.

The Downside Midges – although the shop claims to sell repellent candles that actually work! It can be a bit pricey, particularly on Bank Holiday weekends.

The Facilities Most tents pitch up in the lower third of the slightly sloping site, which also has hard-standing pitches at the top, and a grassy hook-up area for tents and motor homes in the middle. There are clean and plentiful showers, toilets and hand-basin cubicles, a family toilet, shower and baby-change room, and disabled toilet and shower room. A laundry room has washing machines and dryers, and the onsite shop stocks food basics (bring your own fresh fruit and veg) and charges 20p to re-freeze icepacks.

Onsite Fun As well as the adventure playground, there is lots of space between pitches for ball games and running and biking around. If the nature-based ranger activities or orienteering don't appeal, Horrid Henry-types will enjoy forest laser combat.

Offsite Fun There's horse-riding at Friars Hill Stables (01751 432758) at nearby Sinnington (just off the A170) and a small open-air lido is run by volunteers at Helmsley (about 20 minutes away) and opens mid-July to early September. The site is also an ideal base for exploring the North York Moors National Park (www.visitnorthyorkshiremoors.co.uk) and the Yorkshire coast, with Scarborough and Whitby both about 25 miles away, and York (35 miles away) is do-able as a day trip.

If it Rains Castle Howard, an impressively grand stately home (01653 648444; www.castlehoward. co.uk) is about 20 miles away. The North Yorkshire Moors Railway (01751 472508; www.nymr.co.uk) offers nostalgic steam train rides from nearby Pickering (7 miles away) across the moors to Whitby.

Food & Drink The local pubs are both a good walk (particularly with small children), but the nearest options are, in one direction, home-cooked food at the New Inn at Cropton (01751 417330; www.newinncropton.co.uk) and in the other, fresh local produce at the child- and pet-friendly Blacksmith's Country Inn at Hartoft (01751 417331).

Nanny State Alert There is a playground, which may not be suitable for small ones unsupervised – keeping an eye on them might be quite difficult when they've hared off with 20 others to play manhunt dobby!

Getting There By car, from the A170 between Pickering and Kirkbymoorside, turn off at the sign for Wrelton, Cropton and Rosedale. After passing through Cropton (ignoring the sign to Keldy Forest Lodges), keep going down the road, over a small bridge and then turn right into the forest signed 'Spiers House', opposite a cottage on your left. Travelling east on the A170 from Thirsk, avoid the long and very steep hill at Sutton Bank by taking the signposted caravan route via Coxwold.

Public Transport A Moors Bus seasonal service runs direct to the site from Pickering every day during the summer school holidays, but only summer Sundays and Bank Holidays outside this time (01845 597000; www.moors.uk.net/moorsbus).

Open The site is open March–Jan, but is hoping to move to a 50-week season from 2009.

The Damage The cost varies depending when you visit, but a family of 4 pay £20 per night for a standard pitch at the weekend in high season, or £24 on a Bank Holiday weekend. Standard pitches do not include hook-ups.

Spiers House Campsite, Cropton, Pickering, North Yorkshire YO18 8ES

t 08451 308224 (bookings) 01751 417591 (site) | w www.forestholidays.co.uk | 50 on the map

rosedale abbey

Fancy playing Tarzan? It's not exactly in the jungle,
but this site does have lots of rope-swings over the river.
And when your kids have had enough of that, they can try
a little dam-building, tree-climbing, stepping-stone-
jumping – or just plain paddling.

This really is a lovely spot for camping. The site meanders along the banks of the tree-lined river, which, if you're lucky, you can pitch right next to, in a valley surrounded by sweeping hillside moors. And the pretty village of Rosedale Abbey is right there close by. There is no abbey as such, but the village does have plenty on offer, including lots of yummy food, with a deli and two tea rooms around the green, as well as a couple of pubs.

Don't be put off by the somewhat corporate entrance to the campsite – this is not like the Flower of May's other holiday-park-style sites. It does have holiday cottages, statics and tourers, but there are two tent-only fields – and the coolest part of the site is the smaller and quieter of the two, right at the end of the site.

Kids will probably disagree with this assessment, as the tents-only camping field enjoys the widest, shallowest part of the river, where they can carry out all sorts of exploits involving dams, trees, rope-swings and water.

And if, after you've worked your way through this list, you want more, there's the high-wire forest adventure course at Go Ape! in Dalby Forest.

rosedale abbey

The Upside Riverside fun in a picturesque setting.

The Downside Purists will object to the tourers and statics. It can get busy at peak periods, so avoid Bank Holidays if you want peace and tranquillity.

The Facilities Tents pitch up on unmarked pitches (although the site does have some rules about how much space to leave between tents) in the smaller tents-only field, which also has a pond, or the larger tents-only field, which has some pitches with hook-ups. There are 2 toilet/shower blocks with 7 toilets, 5 showers, 5 hand basins for women, and 4 toilets, urinals, 5 showers and 5 hand basins for men in each. Each block has an external toilet, a washing-up area with 2 sinks and a disabled/baby-changing room. One block has a laundry with a washing machine and dryer. The site charges 20p to re-freeze icepacks (proceeds to charity). The small shop, selling a few basics and sweets, is open 8am–6pm (8am–8pm Fridays and Saturdays). Even the family pooch is catered for, with rather splendid views from the 3-acre dog-walking field.

Onsite Fun Most kids seem to prefer the natural playground – the river – but there is also a large playing field for ball games (with basketball hoop), and a play area with climbing frame, 2 slides (a high one and a smaller one), monkey bars and an outdoor table-tennis table.

Offsite Fun Abbey Stores in the village (01751 417475; www.abbeytearoom.co.uk) is the National Park Information Point, hiring out bikes and selling maps and books of short walks. Blakey Ridge on the coast-to-coast walk is popular for its views over the valley, although you might want to drive up the hill and start from there. Further afield, tree-mendous fun can be had by older kids at Go Ape! in Dalby (www.goape.co.uk).

If it Rains Travel back in time and about 4 miles to Ryedale Folk Museum (01751 417367; www.ryedalefolkmuseum.co.uk) in Hutton le Hole to find out about Ryedale's heritage, and how folk lived here in Georgian, Victorian and Tudor times.

Food & Drink You won't starve in Rosedale. The site is a 2-minute walk from the village centre, consisting mainly of pubs and tea shops. Abbey Stores (see Offsite fun) sells the basics and has a tea room, while there is a deli counter and ice creams at Molly's Farm Shop and tea room (01751 417468; www.mollysofrosedale.co.uk). The child-friendly Coach House (01751 417208) is opposite the campsite and will happily split an adult meal onto 2 plates for kids.

Nanny State Alert There is a river nearby. Although generally low and shallow, it can run fast when it's high after heavy rain.

Getting There By car, from the A170 between Pickering and Kirkbymoorside, turn off at Wrelton and follow signs to Cropton and Rosedale. Follow the signs to Rosedale through Cropton and Hartoft and keep going until you come into Rosedale Abbey village. Pass the Caravan Club site on your left and keep going until you see the 'Rosedale' sign, also on the left.

Public Transport There is a Moors bus service to Rosedale from Pickering (01845 597000; www.moors.uk.net) and the North Yorkshire Moors Railway runs from Pickering a few miles away.

Open Easter–end Oct half term. Cottages all year.

The Damage £14 (low season), £16 (mid-season) or £19 (high season) per night for a family of 4 with a tent and a car. A pet per pitch allowed. No all-male or all-female groups permitted.

Rosedale Abbey Country Caravan Park, Rosedale Abbey, Nr Pickering, North Yorkshire YO18 8SA

| t 01751 417272 | w www.flowerofmay.com | **51** on the map |

masons

What a treat! A campsite that's actually run
by campers who know all about choosing a great site.
The river is great for wading and fishing and you can
make a dramatic river-entry via a rope-swing,
handily located on the bank.

In the heart of the Yorkshire Dales, by the banks of the Wharfe, down the road from two good pubs – Masons is so good that even the owners still camp here. When their favourite campsite in the Yorkshire Dales came up for sale, Georgie and Grant bought Masons, and set about scrubbing up an already-popular site.

You no longer have to walk a mile to the nearest shop. Since Burnsall's Shop on the Green went mobile, Dirk arrives each morning with goodies including fresh croissants, eggs and locally made sausages and bacon. At summer weekends he's back in the evening with BBQs and the meat to put on them.

The wide and mainly shallow river runs at the bottom of the two camping fields, with large, flat stones for paddling around. Try your hand at fly-fishing – while the kids happily pass the time catching crayfish with a bucket and net.

The flat camping fields have plenty of space for kite-flying, football, cricket and rounders, and lots of families bring lilos and dinghies. Although the site has open views over an area of outstanding natural beauty, Grant says that campers make straight for the steep hill over the road for an even better vista.

masons

The Upside On the banks of a river, with open views over the Yorkshire Dales and lots of space for games, with 2 great pubs nearby.

The Downside With only 40 pitches on one field, and restrictions on the second limiting camping to 28 days a year, this site gets booked up well in advance – although if you are hikers or (pedal) bikers you won't be turned away.

The Facilities You can pitch wherever you like in the main camping field, which caters for tents, camper vans and tourers, with 30 hook-ups. In the second field, which is open most summer weekends, tents pitch up along the river bank, leaving plenty of space for ball games in the rest of the large field. The washing-up room has 4 sinks, there are 5 showers (including one in a family room) and the toilet blocks each have 3 toilets and 3 hand basins. Tins, glass and paper are recycled. As well as the mobile shop, the site sells eggs (you can see the free-range chickens wandering happily around the site) and camping equipment, and there are 10 rent-a-tents – pre-erected and fully equipped, ranging from 2- to 9-person size. Plans are already in hand for tipis, a washing machine and dryer in a drying room, and fire boxes for campfires are under investigation.

Onsite Fun Paddling and jumping in the river, crayfishing, ball games and tree-climbing. The onsite chickens and ducks are popular with younger children.

Offsite Fun Footpaths lead directly from the bottom of the site along the river to Burnsall, which is a popular picnicking and swimming spot, as well as to Appletreewick and Barden Bridge. Bolton Abbey (01751 432758), with stepping stones over the river,

walks, tea shops, cafés and the Embsay and Bolton Abbey Steam railway station (01756 710614; www.embsayboltonabbeyrailway.org.uk) is just up the road.

If it Rains A notice board next to the showers tells you what's on at local cinemas, and Stump Cross Caverns in Nidderdale (01756 752780; www.stumpcrosscaverns.co.uk) are another good rainy-day option.

Food & Drink The 2 pubs in Appletreewick both serve food and are family-friendly. The New Inn (01756 720252) has a selection of quirky beers, while the 16th-century Craven Arms (01756 720270; www.craven-cruckbarn.co.uk) has log fires, gas lamps and stone-flagged floors.

Nanny State Alert The usual warnings about supervising children near water apply, particularly if dinghies and lilos are involved.

Getting There From the A59 between Skipton and Harrogate, turn north on the B6160 at Bolton Abbey, signposted 'Grassington'. After about 3 miles take the first right after Barden Tower, signposted 'Appletreewick' and continue for around 2 miles to a T-junction. Then turn left into Appletreewick village and continue until, less than a mile on, you reach Masons Campsite at the foot of the hill on the left.

Public Transport The number 74 bus runs 4 times a day (except Sundays) between Ilkley and Grassington.

Open Mid-March–end Oct.

The Damage A family pitch is £19.50, including one car. Dogs go free (max 2 per pitch), but must be kept under strict control.

Masons, Ainhams House, Appletreewick, Skipton, North Yorkshire BD23 6DD

| t | 01756 720275 | w | www.masonscampsite.co.uk | 52 | on the map |

rukin's park lodge

Fire and water are the main attractions at this
site: campfires on the grassy river bank and tumbling
waterfalls abound. Come nightfall, star-gazers will be more
than impressed by the beautiful clear sky.

The river and waterfalls may be the main attraction for kids on this site, making the riverside pitches in the long narrow field at the bottom of the farm the most popular. But the views from the higher fields over the moors are spectacular. And even if you don't get to pitch on the river bank, Keld (meaning 'running water') has no fewer than five waterfalls surrounding the village, so you can always pack up a picnic or set off to find a perfect waterside spot for a great afternoon of splashing around and paddling.

Campfires are allowed here – another major plus. A lot of farmers won't permit them because they ruin the grass. John and Barbara, who farm the land in a way that's sensitive to the environment, were also concerned that campfires were contributing to the erosion of the river bank. But John has come up with his own solution: four-legged fire boxes. These keep the fires off the ground: happy farmers and happy campers.

And if anyone's still awake when the campfire's embers finally fade, it's time to turn to the night sky for a truly awesome star display before tucking the kids up into their sleeping bags.

rukin's park lodge

The Upside Campfires by the river bank in Swaledale – pronounced by walking guru Wainwright as the most beautiful Yorkshire Dale.

The Downside The site can get overwhelmed on summer weekends – there was only 1 shower when we visited, although an upgrade is planned, and it's a long walk to the loo from the riverside pitches. Also midges – but Barbara stocks a secret-formula body spray, which keeps 'em away.

The Facilities As well as the long narrow field by the river, with the most sought-after pitches, there is a large sloping field, and John can open up other fields as overflow. These actually have better views and more space for games than those by the river. There are no marked pitches, but John or Barbara will often help you find a good spot. There is only 1 shower, 3 toilets with hand basins (1 for women, 1 for men and 1 for either) and a washing-up sink, although there are plans to extend the facilities. The tea shop at the site (open 8.30am–6pm) sells drinks plus bacon rolls and egg-on-toast-type food, and stocks groceries and camping basics. It also sells logs and marshmallows – in case you've forgotten these essential ingredients – as well as footpath maps and guides.

Onsite Fun It's only a short walk to the nearest falls, and kids can swim in the shallow pools along the river, paddle, mess about with fishing nets from the flattish rocks, or play on the rope-swing on the small 'beach' just offsite. By evening they should be ready to sit and toast marshmallows, before drifting off under the stars.

Offsite Fun Down river, you can reach the most spectacular falls (Kisdon Force) via Corpse Way, once used to carry bodies to consecrated ground.

The pool beneath Wain Wath Falls, a mile from Keld upriver, is popular for swimming and picnicking.

If it Rains Head into Hawes (about 8 miles/half an hour's drive), where the Dales Countryside Museum (01969 666210) is housed in the old railway station and has interactive displays on life in the Yorkshire Dales. The Wensleydale Creamery Visitor Centre (01969 667664; www.wensleydale-creamery.co.uk) has a museum, viewing gallery, cheese shop and restaurant.

Food & Drink A short walk up the road, Keld Lodge (01748 886259) has a restaurant and also does bar meals, while Tan Hill Inn (01833 628246; www.tanhillinn.com), about 4 miles away, claims to be Great Britain's highest pub, with resident sheep, ducks, dogs and cats. Head into Muker for more pubs and tea shops.

Nanny State Alert In the river, some of the rocks can be slippery, the water is deep in places and there is a waterfall not far away.

Getting There From the west, leave the M6 at junction 38 and take the A685 to Kirkby Stephen. Turn right on the B6259 then left onto the B6270 to Keld. Turn left into the village and you will see signs to the campsite. From the east, leave the A1 by the A6108 (or A6136 which meets the A6108) and turn left onto the B6270. Stay on this road until Keld, and turn right to go into the village and campsite.

Public Transport A bus to Keld leaves Richmond train station 3 times a day.

Open All year.

The Damage Prices per night are £5 adults and £2.50 for children.

Rukin's Park Lodge, Keld, Richmond, North Yorkshire DL11 6LJ

| t 01748 886274 | w www.rukins-keld.co.uk | 53 on the map |

dolphinholme house farm

Forget about the Nanny State and think
about the Nanny Goat instead. Come and meet the
real Billy Goats Gruff and let your kids be kids in a
1920s farmhouse-style 'tent', on a complete
working goat dairy farm.

Dolphinholme House Farm has been in John Gorst's family since the 1930s, sitting at the western edge of the Trough of Bowland, a truly beautiful part of the world, just south of the Lake District. Seven spacious, and very comfortable 'tents' – they have raised wooden floors and beds with mattresses, pillows and even duvets – are set out on the edge of 35 acres of woodland, overlooking a 10-acre field. The River Wyre, fringed by a line of trees at the bottom of the field, seems to be the only thing rushing by in this peaceful spot.

The emphasis here is on good old-fashioned fun, and the site offers plenty of opportunities for this – swimming, paddling and pottering around with fishing nets in the river, or just picnicking on its banks, climbing trees, running about in the fields and climbing on bales of hay. And in the evening, you can take your pick from the simple pleasures of stories around the campfire, reading together or playing games by candlelight.

Children can also learn about life on a farm and where their food comes from by helping with the milking (the farm makes its own goat's cheese), gathering eggs from the henhouse or helping to make pizza or bread in the traditional wood-fired oven.

dolphinholme house farm

The Upside Ready-made, comfortable 'camping' in a beautiful, rural location with good old-fashioned fun a-plenty.

The Downside It can be quiet during the day as families explore the local attractions – although having it all to yourself may not be such a bad thing. Prices reflect that this is a luxurious way to camp.

The Facilities Each tent has a wood-burning stove, flush toilet, cold running water, a worktop, chiller, dining table, chairs and a couple of comfy deckchairs, and there is a picnic table outside, with stone circles for campfires. There are 2 bedrooms and a bunkroom for the kids, and lighting is by oil lamp and candles – there's no electricity. A shower block has 3 hot showers, including a family shower. The honesty shop is always open and well stocked with fruit and veg, Forest of Bowland butter, locally sourced meat, the farm's own cheese and frozen food, including home-cooked frozen ready-meals. There are board games and toys to borrow.

Onsite Fun Kids of the 2-legged variety can play with the 4-legged ones in the barn, which also has a hay mountain for crawling over and a tyre swing, and there are ponies, hens, pigs, rabbits and guinea pigs – so lots of petting opportunities. There's also onsite bike hire (bring your own helmets) and tours of the farm, with trails and footpaths.

Offsite Fun Local attractions include picnicking at Abbeystead reservoir, fishing at Wyreside lakes (01524 791154), or horse-riding at the Bay Horse School of Equitation at Forton (07791 476033), just the other side of the M6. The traditional seaside village of Arnside is a little over half an hour away, 4 miles beyond Morecambe.

If it Rains For younger children, there is a play barn (and tea room) at Old Holly Farm (01524 791200;

www.oldhollyfarm.com) while Lancaster Castle (01524 64998; www.lancastercastle.com) and the Maritime Museum (01772 534075) are other good wet-weather options, both about 7 miles away.

Food & Drink Wallings Farm near Cockerham (01524 793781; www.wallingsfarm.co.uk) has an ice-cream parlour as well as a nice coffee shop and a good restaurant. The Fleece at Dolphinholme (01524 791233; www.thefleeceonline.com) serves hearty pub grub while the Bay Horse at Forton offers gastro-pub fare (01524 791204; www.bayhorseinn.com).

Nanny State Alert There's a river. Some people may need reminding to wash their hands after playing with animals. As it's a working farm there are agricultural vehicles moving around.

Getting There Leave the M6 at junction 33 taking the first exit off the roundabout. Take an immediate left up Hampson Lane to a T-junction, and turn right. Follow the road for 2 miles to a crossroads with the Fleece pub in front and turn left to Dolphinholme village, then continue to the first of a set of mini roundabouts. Take a sharp right into Lower Dolphinholme, go through the village and take the first lane on your left after leaving the village up a hill. You will be provided with full directions when you reserve your tent.

Public Transport A taxi from Lancaster railway station is the sensible public transport option.

Open Easter–late Oct.

The Damage Tents sleep 6 people (max 5 adults) and cost (including linen rental) £195–495 for a 4-night midweek stay, or £245–545 for a 3/4-night weekend stay, depending on when you visit.

Dolphinholme House Farm, Dolphinholme, Lancaster, Lancashire LA2 9DJ

t 01524 791469 or 07900 577517   w www.featherdown.co.uk   on the map

four winds

OK, so the Lake District is in the north-west,
not the Wild West. But the changeable weather in
these parts may tempt you to try out some
ready-made camping in fully equipped
traditional Sioux tipis.

First-time campers? Your family not completely convinced that camping in the Lake District is such a great idea? Then Four Winds might just be the perfect place for your first under-canvas foray. Although this is more back-to-nature, wild camping than the luxury 'glamping' other not-quite-camping sites offer, you won't find you have to struggle with a wet tent here!

Six tipis, decorated atmospherically with native North American symbols of animals and dream sequences, have been assembled in groups, or stand alone, in 20 acres of private, hillside woodland. Through the trees you can glimpse Lake Windermere – and a short walk across the road at the bottom of the woods and through the National Trust's Fell Foot Park takes you to its shores.

You pretty much have the woods to yourselves because there are never more than 25 people here at any one time. And depending what time of year it is, you can enjoy walking through them full of spring flowers, or go foraging for succulent wild cherries or blackberries.

But the real attraction for the kids will probably be the unforgettable experience of camping in the tipis themselves – so don't forget to take your children's cowboys-and-indians costumes!

four winds

The Upside Ready-made, back-to-nature tipi-camping in private woodland, within easy reach of Lake Windermere.

The Downside A bit of traffic noise. Although it's very accessible, the woodland is just off the road between Newby Bridge and Ulverston, and only a mile from the A590, which takes traffic to the Western Lakes. As to be expected, it's expensive compared with conventional camping.

The Facilities The tipis sleep up to 6 people and come fully equipped with air mats, rugs, cushions, candle lanterns, gas cooker and cool box. Crockery, cutlery and cooking equipment is provided, along with a table and bench and a box of toys and books. Outside, where (to be authentic) cooking and eating should take place, there are camping tables and chairs, hammocks and chimeneas, firebowls or braziers. All you need to bring is a torch or camping lamp, freezer packs, sleeping bags, towels and tea towels. A small toilet block has 2 female toilets with 2 washbasins, 1 male toilet with washbasin, a washing-up area with 2 sinks, and a shower (complete with woodland view). There's no shop here, but Forest Fuels at the bottom of the woods sells timber and charcoal.

Onsite Fun Twenty acres of woods to explore, and children's toys and games provided.

Offsite Fun A short walk across the road takes you into the National Trust's Fell Foot Country Park, which has direct access to Lake Windermere for swimming, paddling and boating – you can rent rowing-boats here. There's also a playground and a tea shop with a small nature room.

If it Rains Just across the lake (follow the signs through Newby Bridge) is the Lakes Aquarium (01539 530153; www.aquariumofthelakes.co.uk), with its virtual dive bell, and the Lakeland and Haverthwaite Steam Railway station (01539 531594; www.lakesiderailway.co.uk).

Food & Drink Stock up at Bowness or Ulverston, both about 15 minutes' drive away, and for local pubs, try the lakeside Swan Hotel (01539 531681; www.swanhotel.com) at Newby Bridge for soup and sandwiches (children welcome). The Masons Arms (01539 568486; www.masonsarmsstrawberrybank. co.uk), about 3 miles away at Strawberry Bank on the way to Bowness, has a menu including both traditional Cumbrian and modern gastro dishes.

Nanny State Alert The site is in hillside woodland so there are some edges you need to keep small children away from. The water source is spring-fed, so the site's health and safety policy advises boiled drinking water; you may want to take bottled water.

Getting There From the M6 junction 36 follow the A590 towards Barrow for 10 miles. At a roundabout with junctions for Newby Bridge, Barrow, Ulverston, Bowness and Windermere, take the right junction that skirts Lake Windermere. Approximately a mile down the road on the right is a sign for 'Gummers How'. Take the next right, turning into the wood yard of Lakeland Forest Fuels. The tipis are in the woods behind the yard.

Public Transport A 618 bus from Ambleside and Windermere stops at Fell Foot around 5 times a day (0871 200 2233; www.stagecoachbus.com).

Open Open all year.

The Damage An 18-foot tipi costs from £190 (for a Friday/Sat night visit for 4 people), to £670 for 6 people for a week. Children under 4 are free, and prices are the same year round.

---

4 Winds Lakeland Tipis, Lakeland Forest Fuels, Fell Foot Wood, Newby Bridge, Cumbria LA12 8NN

| t 01539 823755 | w www.4windslakelandtipis.co.uk | 55 on the map |

fisherground

Marshmallow-toasting? Check. Water? Check. Playgrounds? Check. Trains? Check – all the things that make camping really cool for kids. And you can actually arrive at the site's own station by steam locomotive.

This is a great site for kids. It ticks all their campsite boxes and probably a few more besides. Campfires are not only allowed, but positively encouraged in selected areas, with bags of logs complete with kindling and firelighters sold onsite each evening. Owner Mike takes a 'We like you to succeed' approach – just don't forget to pack the marshmallows.

The first thing that meets you on arrival is the pond, fed by a stream and usually full of children playing on tyre rafts – it makes a perfect focal point for kids to get to know each other. The playground has everything your young outward-bounder desires in the way of zip wires, climbing frames, tyre-rope-swings and adventure courses. And there's an added extra: the site sits along the route of the Ravenglass and Eskdale steam railway line – a fab way to arrive if you're coming by public transport. So if you've walked into the nearby hamlet of Boot and there are some tired little legs as a result, hop on board for a scenic choo-choo trip back to camp.

For the adults, the site is in the heart of the Eskdale valley, a quieter part of the Lake District, far from its hustle and bustle. Rugged, bracken-clad fells, woods and grazing sheep provide a splendid backdrop to rest your eyes on when you do eventually find time to relax.

fisherground

The Upside A children's paradise with scenery for the adults. And no tourers.

The Downside It's at least an hour's drive from the M6.

The Facilities Unmarked pitches in 2 main areas: a larger field nearest to the children's playground, and a smaller, quieter field nearest to the toilet/shower block, with wheel rims for campfires. The women's toilet block has 4 hand basins, 4 showers (50p-coin operated), and 5 loos; the men's are the same (except 4 toilets and 3 urinals), with 6 washing-up sinks outside. There is a washing machine, 3 tumble-dryers, a boot-dryer and freezer. No shop onsite, but you can buy logs, kindling and firelighters. Noise after 10.30pm is not allowed.

Onsite Fun Lots! As well as the playground and pond, there are rocks and trees for climbing on and plenty of space for ball games – there's a field next door for bigger games.

Offsite Fun If you manage to drag the kids off the site, go by steam train to Ravenglass, or make the short trip to Dalegarth. From here you can walk into Boot or up to Stanley Force, following the tumbling beck up to the waterfall. A short walk towards Eskdale Green takes you along the River Esk, where a shallow area by the bridge is a good spot for a quick, if chilly, dip.

If it Rains In the pond! Kids who stay here don't seem to mind getting wet. But if you want to get out of the rain, take a tour of Eskdale Mill in Boot (01946 723335; www.eskdalemill.co.uk), one of the few remaining 2-wheel water corn mills. The mill also has a small honesty library.

Food & Drink There is no shop onsite. The nearest is in Eskdale Green for basics (www.eskdalestores.co.uk) and there are 2 good pubs for food in Boot –

the Brook House Inn (01946 723288; www.brookhouseinn.co.uk) and the Boot Inn (01946 723224; www.bootinn.co.uk).

Nanny State Alert The kids will be straight into the pond, rain or shine, before you've had a chance to even pitch your tent.

Getting There Beware of using sat-nav if you want to avoid taking the white-knuckle ride over Hardknott and Wrynose Passes. From the south, leave the M6 at junction 36 and follow signs for Barrow, then 3 miles past Newby Bridge turn right towards Workington on the A5092. Keep on this road for around 10 miles, then beyond Broughton-in-Furness, turn right at traffic lights towards Ulpha. Turn left in Ulpha village to the steep hill signed 'Eskdale', follow the fell road to the King George IV pub and turn right to Boot. The campsite is 300 metres on the left. From the north, leave the M6 at junction 43 towards Workington/Cockermouth on the A595 then turn onto the A5086 to Cleator Moor and Egremont. Rejoin the A595, passing Egremont and Gosforth and driving through Holmrook. Turn left after the garage to Eskdale Green, follow the road to the next junction and turn right, then go through Eskdale village to the King George IV pub and turn left to Boot.

Public Transport There are no buses to Fisherground, so the steam train is the only public-transport option. Although it is a bit more expensive than a standard bus or train, why not arrive in style?

Open Early March–late Oct.

The Damage Adults are charged £5, children £2.50, vehicles £2.50 and dogs £1 per night. No bookings are taken.

Fisherground Campsite, Fellside Cottage, Eskdale, Holmrook, Cumbria CA19 1TF

t 01946 723349   w www.fishergroundcampsite.co.uk   56 on the map

seal shore

Jostle for elbow-room on a private beach with the
seals and sea birds, while you keep a wary eye out for
sharks in the water. Seal Shore's a great site for teaching
your kids what fish fingers look like before they go
into the factory.

If you had to squeeze the whole of Scotland onto the lid of a shortbread tin, you'd end up with something like this little island. Arran is famous for being Scotland in miniature. It has wild highland hills in the north of the island, rolling farmland in the south and is dotted with standing stones.

Seal Shore's on the southern tip of the island, looking out towards the Pladda Lighthouse and Ailsa Craig (no, not a Scottish actress but a 300-metre-high rocky plug of an extinct volcano). Although its private stretch of beach is a bit rocky, there's a sandy version a few hundred metres away, if your kids prefer building sandcastles to teaching seals to clap or balance balls on the ends of their noses. And the sharks, just so you know, are the basking variety, so are more interested in cruising about looking cool than re-enacting scenes from *Jaws*, with your children as extras.

Onsite, there are grass-based activities to enjoy, like running and falling over. And because the place is quite compact, it provides a great location to practise your close-combat skills. Or you can dig a big hole in the sand and try to tunnel through the Earth. But it would bring you out 600 miles south of New Zealand, so it's probably not a very sensible idea.

seal shore

The Upside Wild times with the sea life on a stunning private beach.

The Downside Arran's not much more than a collection of seaside towns with loads of hills in between, so it's not much fun when it rains. The site can also get pretty windy, so sturdy tents are advisable.

The Facilities Award-winning showers (you mean there are awards for showers?), set in a neat and well-maintained white-washed block. It's warm as well, which is a bonus, and it has baby-changing facilities. Elsewhere there's a campers' day room with a TV and a kitchen area, which is handy when the wind's up.

Onsite Fun Very much based around the shore, with its wildlife variety and the nearby sandy beach.

Offsite Fun Try something different and go gorge-walking. It's wet and it's wild and involves climbing, scrambling, jumping and plunging and the odd bit of doggy-paddling up, down and around watery gorges. It's quite pricey at £40 for adults and £25 for children aged 6–17 (it's not suitable for the under-6s), but it's pretty exhilarating. Three-hour trips are run by the Arran Adventure Company (01770 302244; www.arranadventure.com).

If it Rains Arran is so geared towards the great outdoors that you'd best keep your fingers crossed it stays dry. There is a museum at Brodick (the Arran Heritage Museum; 01770 302636; www. arranmuseum.co.uk), which runs various practical demonstrations, like how to shoe a horse, which is both handy and informative. Alternatively, there is the Auchrannie Hotel (01770 302234; www.auchrannie. co.uk), which has an attached leisure complex, including a pool. But then you've probably had enough of the water.

Food & Drink There's a good campers' kitchen at the site if you want to cook your own. Get your supplies at the Co-op in Brodick (turn right from the ferry and it's a few hundred metres up the road on the left). Or the lazy option is to walk all of 20 metres from the site to the Kildonan Hotel (01770 820207; www.kildonanhotel.com), which has a great little bar looking out across the garden to the sea and a more formal restaurant called the Stone Garden.

Nanny State Alert You mean apart from the sharks? Well, it's a beach and there are waves and water, so best keep an eye out and ensure you've brought your waterwings. Most of the wildlife will be more scared of your kids than your kids will be of them. The same may be true of some of the adults. The site's fairly self-contained and well away from the (very quiet) road, but one thing to watch out for is anorak-snagging barbed wire on top of the fences.

Getting There From Brodick take the B841 south for about 12 miles. Turn left at the sign for Kildonan and follow the road down the hill towards the sea. The campsite is down a side road on the left next door to the Kildonan Hotel.

Public Transport There is a regular bus service which stops 50 metres from the site.

Open March–Oct.

The Damage Adults are £6 and children aged 6–15 are £3. Under-5 get off Scot-free (as is their wont). The cost of tent is £1–3, depending on size.

Seal Shore Camping & Touring Site, Kildonan, Isle of Arran KA27 8SE

| t 01770 820320 | w www.campingarran.com | 57 on the map |

glenbrittle

Try some remote seashore-camping on the remote
side of the already remote Isle of Skye, under the watchful
eye of the Black Cuillins. You can collect some mussels for
supper and cook 'em up on a beach fire, while watching
the Milky Way appear in the evening sky.

If your kids think the Milky Way's just the name of a chocolate bar, then Glenbrittle's the place to show them the real thing. There aren't many places in Britain where you can still see the white ribbon of stars in the night sky, but this remote campsite, seven miles down a single track, is one of them.

Apart from the stars, the main attractions are the sheltered bay, with its long curving beach and the fact that it's an ideal base to tackle the hills of the Black Cuillins. You won't want to attempt the really serious stuff (you'll find you really need ropes and loads of metal thingies for that), but it's a great place to introduce kids to the hills.

If nothing else there are fantastic views of the bay if you clamber up the side of the hill above the site. But even if you fancy nothing more than a bit of R&R, you can leave the kids to play hide-and-seek among the alternating patches of long grass and putting-green pitches that make up most of the site.

Or, instead of cowboys and indians, give them a Scottish history lesson by getting them to play Jacobites and Redcoats. You might need to mug up on your local history before you do, though.

glenbrittle

The Upside You'll find it down 7 miles of single-track road on the remote coast of the Isle of Skye.

The Downside The site is a bit let down by its washing facilities and the fact that you have to boil the water.

The Facilities They're pretty basic. There's a rustic wash-block, which has long been rumoured to be on the point of an upgrade, but never quite seems to manage it. The showers won't get you very wet either. To top it all, you're advised to boil the tap water, even for cleaning your teeth, so it's a good idea to take plenty of the bottled variety along with you. However, there's a well-stocked shop onsite for all the basics.

Onsite Fun For a start there's a lengthy beach, which is sheltered enough to be safe for even toddlers to have a paddle. It's also a potential source of a meal as you can collect mussels on the beach at low tide. Apart from that there's just acres of long green grass and the allure of the hills to keep the kids running around for hours.

Offsite Fun Head up to the Fairy Pools, the magical (but chilly) series of dipping pools in the side of the Cuillins a few miles back up the track that leads to the site. A wet suit's advisable for softies (or people from England).

If it Rains This is tricky as the site is very remote and even the Sligachan Hotel (see Food & Drink) is 15 miles away. The best idea, though he's nearly 30 miles away, is to visit the local clan chief Hugh

MacLeod of MacLeod at his great Hebridean stronghold of Dunvegan Castle (01470 521206; www.dunvegancastle.com). Ask to see the Fairy Flag, a magical flag that is reputed to summon a fairy army when it's waved. Like so many magical things, it can only be used 3 times and has already been waved twice. Who knows when it might need to be used again? The castle's open April–Oct and costs £20 for a family ticket for 2 adults, 2 children and a guide book.

Food & Drink Seven miles down a single-track road means this really is self-catering territory. Fires are allowed on the beach, so steaming some self-collected mussels is a fun way to eat. If you really need a bit of civilisation (and someone else to do the washing-up) head to the Sligachan Hotel (01478 650202; www.sligachan.co.uk), where there's a swanky restaurant and a cheaper bar-meal option.

Nanny State Alert Apart from having to boil the drinking water, the main issue is the sea. It's reasonably sheltered, but it's still pretty wet.

Getting There Take the A87 to Sligachan and then the A863, turning by the hotel towards Dunvegan. After 5 miles take the B8009 for Carbost and, just before entering the village, turn left onto the single-track road for Glenbrittle.

Open Mid-April–early Oct

The Damage £5 per adult and £3.50 per child (5–16) per night. Dogs £1.

Glenbrittle Campsite, Glenbrittle, Carbost, Isle of Skye IV47 8TA

t 01478 640404

58 on the map

morvich

An arch enemy of Harry Potter? No, a campsite
from which to explore the great outdoors. In the shadow of
the Five Sisters of Kintail, in the Scottish highlands near
Skye, huff and puff through the heather and have
yourself some outdoor adventure.

If you don't want to raise a crop of sofa spuds with over-developed gaming thumbs, drag your kiddies up to Morvich and spring-clean their lungs with some pure fresh air. At this little patch of the Scottish Highlands there's no such thing as indoors. Only outdoors. It's a secluded spot, ideal for the quiet life, but with some brassy adventures waiting outside your tent flaps.

The campsite's a long caber-toss from the shores of Loch Duich, with its dramatic castle, recognisable from many a tin of shortbread. The sea loch's a popular spot for sea-kayakers and is probably the best place for dramatic views of the Five Sisters of Kintail. They're not, as you might think, a coven of witches, but a range of mountains, drawn in crayon colours of purple, brown and green, that make for a serious hill-walking challenge.

But the campsite, run by the Caravan Club, is equally a lovely little patch of greenery in which to while away the days, doing nothing more than drinking in the views of the last of the Five Sisters. And getting your crayons out if you fancy trying to capture it on paper.

morvich

The Upside Lungfuls of fresh Highland air and the chance to stride across open hills.

The Downside Relative to the size of the site, the 2 camping areas are fairly compact.

The Facilities What you expect from the Caravan Club – excellent, clean and plentiful. There are warm wash-rooms with good strong hot showers and also a special family bathroom for the under-4s (accompanied by a parent or guardian, of course). There are also plenty of laundry and washing-up facilities and – handy this – a drying room. However in the camping area the only cooking area is a covered wooden table.

Onsite Fun Smaller kids can cycle or skate around the site in safety (except in the vicinity of the wash-block), but other than that there's not a great deal to do on the site itself.

Offsite Fun Take a trip to see Britain's tallest free-falling waterfall. The Falls of Glomach are a 7-mile return hike from the end of the road past the campsite, so it's only suitable for older children who can walk there and back over remote countryside. But it's worth the trip to see the 100-metre drop. If you'd rather be on the water than just watching it, the National Trust (08444 932231; kintail@nts.org.uk) runs sea-kayaking taster days from the Morvich centre between April and October. No experience is necessary and it's £40 for adults and £25 for children over 10.

If it Rains On the basis that it can't rain under water, try the glass-bottomed boat that makes trips from Kyle of Lochalsh. The grandly named Seaprobe Atlantis (0800 9804846; www.seaprobeatlantis.com) is Scotland's only semi-submersible, glass-bottomed boat and gives you a fish-eye view of the murky depths of the waters around Skye, including an old Second World War wreck. Two adults and 2 children can enjoy a 1-hour trip for £36. Alternatively you can tour the historic Eilean Donan Castle (01599 555202; www.eileandonancastle.com) and find out about the 1719 Battle of Sheil. It's open mid-March to mid-Nov. A family of 2 adults and 3 children can get in for £10.50.

Food & Drink There's a small shop onsite for all the basics and enclosed BBQs are allowed (but sadly open fires aren't) so you can always cook up something yourself. But if you fancy a bit of posh there's the Kintail Lodge Hotel (01599 511275; www.kintaillodgehotel.co.uk) with a sunny conservatory (sadly sun's not on the à la carte menu) and dining room that serves up tasty treats like pan-seared West Coast scallops or chicken breast stuffed with haggis. There's also a bar-meal option with more standard fare.

Nanny State Alert The site is fairly remote and, although the entrance has a gate which is normally kept closed, it's best to keep an eye that no one wanders out. It would be easy to get lost.

Getting There Just off the A87 between Shiel Bridge and Kyle of Lochalsh. Heading north, turn right just over a mile past Shiel Bridge, heading for Morvich. The site entrance is signposted up a minor road to your right. The entrance is on the left opposite the countryside centre.

Open End March–early Nov.

The Damage Prices vary by season, but a family of 4 can expect to pay £22.10 during peak periods (including Easter).

Morvich Caravan Club Site, Morvich, Inverinate, Kyle IV40 8HQ

| t 01599 511354 | w www.caravanclub.co.uk | 59 on the map |

lazy duck

While the kids play with the ducks, geese
and hens and run rings round the forest of Scots
pine, you can laze away the day in your hammock.
You'd be quackers not to.

It's not often that a campsite boasts that it's 'one of Scotland's smallest', but that's exactly how owners David and Valery like to think of Lazy Duck. Size matters. So the camping area here only has room for four tents at a time and, what's more, in order to maintain the intimate atmosphere of the place, the tents can only be of the one- or two-person variety. So you won't see any big dome tents here. Just snug little places huddled round the chimenea fires at night.

Of course, you don't really want to encourage your kids to be lazy. You want them to play football and hockey, learn the violin and grow up to be PM. But, as they say, a little bit of what you fancy does you good. And nothing beats a bit of laziness for that.

This site's a near-perfect little oasis of tranquillity, shared with some pearly-white but extremely lazy Exhibition English Aylesbury ducks, a couple of Swedish Skane geese and various other furry or feathered friends. It's about as quiet and relaxed a place as you can get while still awake. Not that you're likely to stay that way for long if you try out one of the hammocks on a fine summer's day.

lazy duck

The Upside The perfect place to introduce your kids to the pleasures of laziness.

The Downside A family of 4 or more will need to bring 2 or more small tents rather than 1 big one. Being such a small site, it is essential to book (easily done on the website).

The Facilities As intimate as the site itself. There's a small toilet and wash-room in the main house, along with laundry facilities. If you fancy a shower, grab a solar-warmed bag of water and head for the edge of the forest, where you'll find an open wooden cubicle. It's pretty bracing on a chilly morning, but a great way to start the day. And if you are feeling the chill, there's a snug 2-person sauna onsite.

Onsite Fun The ducks and geese, the pond, the forest, the hammocks and loads of safe space to explore. And if that's not enough, the little fire-stoves (called chimeneas) with help-yourself wood are just begging for you to roast, toast and melt everything from cheese to marshmallows.

Offsite Fun Aviemore is the Chamonix of the Cairngorms – the centre of everything outdoors that goes up and comes back down. Apart from abundant hill-walking opportunities, the area is famed for its mountain- and quad-biking. On water you can sail, paddle, windsurf or fish. Or you can horse-ride, try archery, clay-pigeon shooting or paint-balling. And if that's all too much effort you can take the funicular railway up Britain's sixth-highest mountain, Cairngorm. The best way to make sense of it all is to visit www.visitaviemore.com and take your pick.

If it Rains There's a clue to the weather in these parts – the official Aviemore website has a special section on what to do when it's wet. The pick of an eclectic bunch as far as kids are concerned is the Fun House at Coylumbridge (back down the B970 from Lazy Duck). It's part of the Hilton Hotel (01479 813081) and has indoor mini golf (£3 per person), 10-pin bowling (£2), a soft play area (£2 for under-2s, £4 for ages 2–4, £5 for the over-5s and £1 for adults) and various other attractions, including an American Diner. It's open from 10am each day.

Food & Drink Lazy Duck is the kind of place crying out for you to cook your own food on the open fire. But there are a couple of (lazy) options. One's the Ord Bàn Café in Rothiemurchus (01479 810005), which has omnivore and herbivore sandwich options and deli plates of produce from the Rothiemurchus Estate. There's also a kids' menu with funky things like peanut butter, banana and honey sandwiches (called a 'double-dozer').

Nanny State Alert Keep an eye out around the pond. It's not deep, but it does have sides that would make it difficult for a small child to get out. Also, the geese can snap at pointed fingers, but then, as your kids will know, it's rude to point.

Getting There From Aviemore follow the A95 towards Grantown-on-Spey. After about 8 miles, turn left towards Nethy Bridge. Enter the town down Station Road and do a quick left onto the B970 and then right and you'll find the campsite signposted on the edge of the village off the Tomintoul Road.

Open May–Oct.

The Damage £9 per night for one person and £4 per night for each additional person. No dogs allowed.

Lazy Duck Hostel, Nethy Bridge, Inverness-shire PH25 3ED

t 01479 821642	w www.lazyduck.co.uk	60 on the map

happy campers?

We hope you've enjoyed reading *Cool Camping: Kids* and that it's inspired you to get out there.

The campsites featured in this book are a personal selection chosen by the Cool Camping team. None of the campsites has paid a fee for inclusion, nor was one requested, so you can be sure of an objective choice of sites and honest descriptions.

We have visited hundreds of campsites across the UK to find the 60 in this book, and we hope you like them as much as we do. However, it hasn't been possible to visit every single campsite. So, if you know of a special place that you think should be included in the next edition, we'd like to hear about it.

Send us an email telling us the name and location of the campsite, some contact details and why it's special. We'll credit all useful contributions in the next edition and the best emails will receive a complimentary copy. Thanks and see you out there!

kids@coolcamping.co.uk

acknowledgements

Cool Camping: Kids (1st edition)
Series Concept & Series Editor: Jonathan Knight
Researched, written and photographed by:
Clover Stroud, Jonathan Knight, Andrea Oates,
Alexandra Tilley Loughrey, with additional
contributions by Sophie Dawson and Keith Didcock
Project Manager: Nikki Sims
Produced by Bookworx (Editorial: Jo Godfrey Wood
Design: Peggy Sadler)
Proofreader: Claire Wedderburn Maxwell
Publishing Assistants: Sophie Dawson and
Catherine Greenwood
PR: The Farley Partnership

Published by: Punk Publishing, 3 The Yard, Pegasus
Place, London SE11 5SD

Distributed by: Portfolio Books, 2nd floor,
Westminster House, Kew Road, Richmond, Surrey
TW9 2ND

All photographs © Clover Stroud/Jonathan Knight/
Andrea Oates/Alexandra Tilley Loughrey/Sophie
Dawson/Keith Didcock except the following (all
reproduced with permission; t = top, b = bottom,
r = right, l = left): **10** br © Fisherground: **14** tl ©
Henry Bloomfield: **40, 43** tr, bl © Ruthern Valley
Holidays: **47** tl, br © Apex Pictures/Chris Saville; tr
© Sandra Lane: **48–51** © Belle Tents: **67** tr, bl
© Doone Valley Holidays: **68** tr © Corbis/Mark
Bolton; b, tl © Westermill/Oliver Edwards; **71** t ©
Corbis/Zefa/Simon Plant; bl, br © Oliver Edwards:
122–124, 127 br © Safari Britain: **135** bl, br © NTPL/
David Levenson: **139** © Clippesby Hall/Paul Studd:
152 © Wickedly Wonderful: **154** © Scottie
Ligertwood/Borrowdale Summer Camp: **155**
© Matthew Rawlinson Plant/Mill on the Brue
Activity Centre: **198** © Colin Tilley Loughrey:
210–213 © Graig Wen: **226, 229** tr © Daniel Start:
249 © Daniel Start: **250, 253** br © Masons/Grant and
Georgie; tl, tr, bl © Daniel Start: **254, 257** tr, bl
Daniel Start: **262, 265** tl © Four Winds: **266, 269** tl
© Fisherground: **281** t © Robin McKelvie: **282** b
© David Dean; tl, tr © Robin McKelvie: **285** tr, bl, br
© Robin McKelvie.

Front cover: Noongallas © Jonathan Knight

Many of the photographs featured in this book are
available for licensing. For more information, see
www.coolcamping.co.uk

The publishers and authors have done their best to
ensure the accuracy of all information in *Cool
Camping: Kids*, however, they can accept no
responsibility for any injury, loss, or inconvenience
sustained by anyone as a result of information
contained in this book.

Punk Publishing takes its environmental
responsibilities seriously. This book has been
printed on paper made from renewable sources and
we continue to work with our printers to reduce
our overall environmental impact. Wherever
possible, we recycle, eat organic food and always
turn the tap off when brushing our teeth.

A BIG THANK YOU! Thanks to everyone who has
written and emailed with feedback, comments and
suggestions. It's good to see so many people at one
with the *Cool Camping* ethos. In particular, thanks
to the following readers for telling us about their
favourite places to camp: Ian Bennett, Rob
Boardman, Jennifer Britt, Jessica Evans-Preston,
Liz Hennessey, Mark Hopgoodwaish, Laura Howell,
Helen Jones, Jo Lewis, Georgina Price, Susan
Ruttley, Anna Tutt and Helena Wolska.

Clover Stroud would like to thank the following:
Alexandra Pringle, James Deavin, Andrew Rees,
Jimmy Joe and Dolly Hughes, Emma Hope, Harry
Cory Wright, Brad Steer, Nell Gifford, Rick Stroud,
Rocky Stone, Fiona Whitehouse, Claudia Fitzherbert,
Margy and Alan Hughes, John Rawlings and VW.